THE GREAT CONFLICT
(BETWEEN GOOD AND EVIL)

Why Disease, Suffering and Anguish Abound in the World

SSB Series

Book 3

ADIARI CAPTAIN

The Great Conflict (Between Good and Evil)
Spirit, Soul and Body (SSB) Series: Book 3

Published by Agape Lifecare Books
Pretoria
books@agapelifecare.com

ISBN 978-0-6399980-0-8
eISBN 978-0-6399980-1-5

2 4 6 8 10 9 7 5 3 1

Layout and cover design by Boutique Books
Printed in South Africa by Digital Action

E-Book Format:
The Great Conflict (Between Good and Evil)
(SSB Book 3) is also available in various electronic versions.
To access the ebook format,
visit: http://www.agapelifecare.com/books.

Also, more hardcopies (paperback) of the book can be
obtained from your local bookshops or contact:
http://www.agapelifecare.com/books.

Abbreviations

AMP = Amplified Bible
CEB = Common English Bible
CEV = Contemporary English Version
Chpt = Chapter
ERV = Easy-to-Read Version
ESV = English Standard Version
EXB = Expanded Bible
GNT = Good News Translation
HCSB = Holman Christian Standard Bible
ICB = International Children's Bible
ISV = International Standard Version
KJV = King James Version
LEB = Lexham English Bible

NABRE = New American Bible (Revised Edition)
NASB = New American Standard Bible
NET = New English Translation
NIRV = New International Reader's Version
NIV = New International Version
NKJV = New King James Version
NLV = New Life Version
NLT = New Living Translation
RSV = Revised Standard Version
SSB = Spirit, Soul and Body
TLB = The Living Bible
Voice = The Voice Bible
WYC = Wycliffe Bible

Alphabetical Listing of the 66 books of the Bible and their Abbreviations

Book	Abbreviation	Book	Abbreviation	Book	Abbreviation
Acts	Act.	James	Jam.	Nehemiah	Neh.
Amos	Amo.	Jeremiah	Jer.	Numbers	Num.
1 Chronicles	1Chr.	Job	Job	Obadiah	Oba.
2 Chronicles	2Chr.	Joel	Joe.	1 Peter	1Pet.
Colossians	Col.	John	Joh.	2 Peter	2Pet.
1 Corinthians	1Cor.	1 John	1Joh.	Philemon	Philem.
2 Corinthians	2Cor.	2 John	2Joh.	Philippians	Philip.
Daniel	Dan.	3 John	3Joh.	Proverbs	Pro.
Deuteronomy	Deu.	Jonah	Jon.	Psalms	Psa.
Ecclesiastes	Ecc.	Joshua	Jos.	Revelation	Rev.
Ephesians	Eph.	Jude	Jude	Romans	Rom.
Esther	Est.	Judges	Judg.	Ruth	Rut.
Exodus	Exo.	1 Kings	1Kin.	1 Samuel	1Sam.
Ezekiel	Eze.	2 Kings	2Kin.	2 Samuel	2Sam.
Ezra	Ezr.	Lamentations	Lam.	Songs of Songs	Son.
Galatians	Gal.	Leviticus	Lev.	1 Thessalonians	1The.
Genesis	Gen.	Luke	Luk.	2 Thessalonians	2The.
Habakkuk	Hab.	Malachi	Mal.	1 Timothy	1Tim.
Haggai	Hag.	Mark	Mar.	2 Timothy	2Tim.
Hebrews	Heb.	Matthew	Mat.	Titus	Tit.
Hosea	Hos.	Micah	Mic.	Zechariah	Zec.
Isaiah	Isa.	Nahum	Nah.	Zepheniah	Zep.

CONTENTS

Declaration and Acknowledgment

ALL THE STORIES TOLD IN this book are true-life occurrences. However, the names of the persons involved were changed to preserve the identities of the individuals, except in few cases in which the story has actually been published with the full disclosure of identity with the consent of the owner or has been published in any other public domain.

I want to thank the numerous permissions we received from relevant quarters while compiling the materials for this book. Especially, I want to thank my wife and children who have been the first students I have used to refine most of the thoughts in this book. The principles in this book are not new because principles are eternal laws of creation. However, the unveiling knowledge of some of these principles are quite novel as they came via the creative illumination from the Holy Spirit, the Greatest Teacher, over the more-than-30 years of my spiritual walk with God. My family were usually the first students to practice the illuminated teachings.

Also, my deep appreciation goes to Mr Peterson Kimani for his contribution in the editing of the manuscript. As you study this book, may you find creative illumination that will enrich your life and drive you towards successful accomplishments beyond the confines of your perceived limitation.

PREFACE

At childhood, we all have big dreams. We dream of achieving exploits in various fields of endeavours. However, as we grow up, we find that these dreams do not just become realised. We come into confrontation with giants that contend with such dreams. For me, coming from an average family with some poverty background, I had longed to escape the clutches of poverty. After an encounter with divine direction at the age of 15, my dream plan to conquer poverty was to become a medical doctor.

However, just at the time when my dream was about to materialise, just at the brink of finishing my high (secondary) school, my father, the breadwinner of my family, suddenly died. This was barely two years after deciding to be a medical practitioner! "What a tragedy! What a fate!" many onlookers thought! With that death, financial darkness seemed to prevail and many thought the hope of realising my academic dream died with my dad. Thus, the monstrous giant on the way of realising my medical dream was financial incapacitation.

For Jane, a friend and an accountant, her confronting giant was not financial helplessness but the loss of a disciplined father figure to guide and direct her. Her parents divorced quite early, and she grew up with her sickly grandmother, who couldn't provide the needed strength and direction. Fortunately, her mother was a hardworking woman and she made sure that Jane got all her basic needs met. However, not having a strong father figure in life, according to her, led to her deviating into a rancorous lifestyle as she joined bad companies that influenced her negatively. With such a riotous lifestyle, her childhood dreams of having a godly family appeared dissipated.

Your giants may not be financial monstrosity like mine or lack of parental support like Jane. Yours may be diseases, misfortunes, marital quagmires, et cetera. Some people have attained some levels of progress in line with their heart desires, but they soon realise they cannot advance further, and that they have even begun to deteriorate. All because of opposition!

Indeed, as a result of antagonising giants, many dreams have been stopped and buried. Many have lost all hope of ever realising their heart's desires. In fact, various studies have shown that only about 5 to 10 percent of humanity ever lived to achieve their heart's desires. Why such a high level of failure? Why does evil seem to pervade the world so much that good people suffer for what they were innocent of?

Sadly, many people are unaware that life on earth is warfare. The day a child is born into the world, he or she has been ushered into an age-old conflict between the forces of good and evil. If he knows not how to fight his battles, he will end up among the 90 percent of human casualties. Indeed, there is a warfare that predates human existence. As long as this present world exists, this warfare will continue. We in this era are in the climax of the warfare. The grand design is being progressively unfolded.

This book, which is the third in SSB series, unveils this age-old warfare. It traces the origin of the war, its progressive battles, and the interplaying forces. In this book, you will read about dwellers on earth who have lived many thousands of years before the arrival of man. Based on Biblical truth, you will come to understand that, really, humans were not the first to inhabit the earth. If you study the book with an open mind, you will finally discover the answers to archaeological findings of fossils and artefacts that antedated human existence. Indeed, science is only unravelling the truth of the Scriptures. In this book, the Bible will come alive and you will be surprised to know that most scientific questions that people think are unanswered are in the Bible.

The age-old war started with these pre-human dwellers, and once humans arrived on earth, they were immediately drafted into the war. It is a war between the forces of good and evil. It is the Great Conflict between Good and Evil that shapes the destiny of mankind in all sectors of human endeavour. Whether you realise it or not, you have been drafted into this age-old war immediately you were born, and the direction of your life and your final destiny are determined by your knowledge of this war and how to fight through.

SECTION ONE

THE PRE-HUMAN ERA

CHAPTER 1

BEFORE THE ARRIVAL OF MAN ON EARTH

IN 1924, FOSSILS OF ANATOMICALLY modern humans, the Homo sapiens, were discovered in Singa of Sudan in East Africa, and were dated to be about one hundred and sixty thousand (160 000) years old. They were found to have appearance consistent with the range of phenotypes in modern humans. Again, in 1967, a collection of Homo sapiens bones was discovered at the Omo Kibish sites near the Omo River, in Omo National Park of Ethiopia in East Africa, by a scientific team from the Kenya National Museums directed by Richard Leakey. The bones were dated to be about one hundred and ninety-five thousand (195 000) years old. These findings and some others made scholars to believe that humans originated from East Africa some two hundred thousand (200 000) years ago.

Then, in 2017, a study was published in the journal *Nature* that showed new excavations from an archaeological site, Jebel Irhoud, in Morocco of North Africa. The excavated fossils included the bones of five different individuals including three young adults, an adolescent and a child estimated to be 8 years of age. The facial features of the skulls look like a modern human, but the brain case is very elongated and archaically unlike ours. In other words, they look like us yet they were not exactly us.

Using thermoluminescence dating method, these Homo sapiens fossils were found to be about 300 000 years old, the oldest to be discovered thus far, as at the writing of this manuscript, thereby forcing scientists to widen their cradle of humankind to include the whole of the African continent. What an assumption! What if older Homo sapiens fossils were found in other parts of the world? Will the cradle of mankind then be expanded to cover the entire earth? That is the limitation of present scientific knowledge, which is full of many scientific assumptions.

Indeed, the fossils of Homo sapiens were not the earliest archaeologically discovered forms of life found on earth. In March 2017, remains of microorganisms of at least 3770 million years old have been discovered in the Nuvvuagittuq Supracrustal Belt (NSB), Quebec, Canada, by an international team led by University College London scientists. Tiny filaments and tubes formed by bacteria that lived on iron were found encased in quartz layers. The NSB contains some of the oldest sedimentary rocks on Earth, which likely formed part of an iron-rich deep-sea hydrothermal vent system that provided a habitat for these microorganisms between 3 770 and 4 300 million years ago. The NSB microfossils were the oldest forms of life discovered thus far on earth. Prior to this discovery, the oldest microfossils reported were found in Western Australia and dated at 3 460 million years old, although some scientists believe that they might be non-biological artefacts in the rocks.

THE CONTROVERSY

Thus, there is no doubt that life existed on earth millions of years ago. However, according to the Bible, man is only about 6 000 years old on earth (see SSB Book 4). Was the Bible inaccurate? If the Bible is inaccurate, it means any belief system based on the Bible is a mere religious exercise. It means Judaism and Christianity, which are both based on the Scriptures of the Bible, are fake and deceptive. Above all, it means the atheists and agnostics are correct to believe that there is no God.

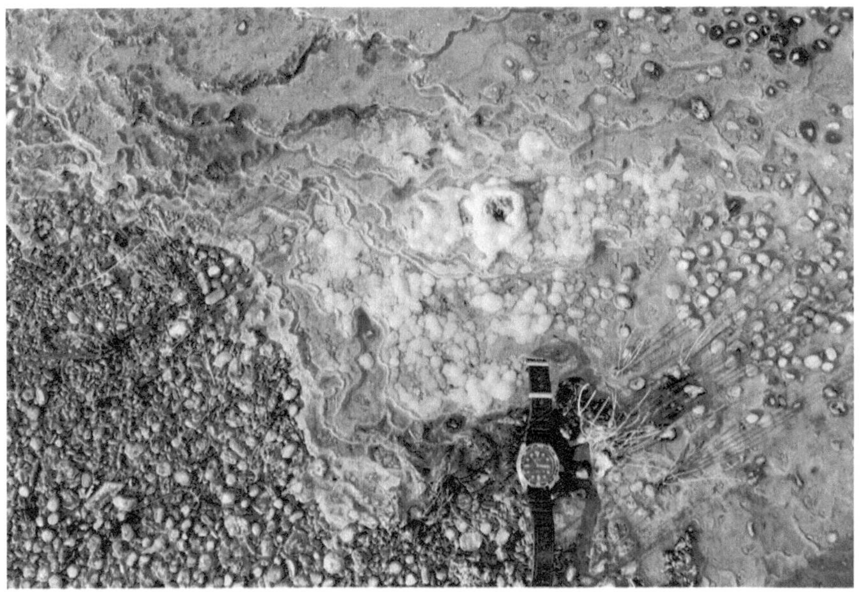

Fig.1: These distinctive wavy globs are a modern-day version of Earth's oldest known life. Stromatolites, microbial mats that thrive on sunlight, have been discovered in Tasmania, Australia, for the first time. Stromatolites first lived around 3.5 billion years ago, and they're rare today. Most live in highly salty marine environments, which makes the Tasmania specimens even more special. They live in freshwater (culled from: Live Science).

CHAPTER 2

THE ETERNAL PURPOSE OF CREATION

IN SSB BOOK 1, IT was shown beyond all doubt that spirituality is a reality, and God is the Author of all, both the physical and the spiritual. Indeed, any man who denies the reality of spiritual existence only beguiles himself; SSB Book 1 emphatically establishes that man is principally a spirit being, possesses a soul, and lives in a physical body.

Interestingly, Genesis chapter one verse one states clearly: *"In the beginning God created the heavens and the earth"* (NIV). This means the followings:

- the heaven and the earth have a beginning
- the heaven and earth were created by God at the beginning era
- God existed before the beginning era.

In other words, besides God, what else existed before the Beginning? How much time was there before the Beginning? As a child, one question I loved to ask was: 'Who was the Father of God and where did God come from?' Often, the elderly people would shout down on me when I asked the question. To them, it was sacrilegious to ask such a question? But the curiosity is still with me now that I am an adult. Interestingly, my kids asked me the same question. However, in this case, I did not shout down at them, but honestly proffered the answers that I know.

THE PRE-BEGINNING

God existed in that time-frame before the Beginning Era. We don't have any human language to describe that time-frame that existed before the Beginning. Let's call that time-frame Pre-Beginning. Thus, besides God, what existed during the Pre-Beginning Era? How did the Pre-Beginning era look like? God was in the Pre-Beginning Era. This we know. But was there any other thing in the Pre-Beginning? The only thing we know certainly that was there with God in the Pre-Beginning Era was *NOTHING*. But what exactly is *NOTHING*? How can we accurately define *NOTHING*? That is the limitation of the human mind and language.

How long was the Pre-Beginning Era? The length of the time-frame of the Pre-Beginning period is *INFINITE*. But 'infinite,' which means endless, may not exactly describe the time-frame of the Pre-Beginning because the Pre-Beginning actually ended at the start of the Beginning Era.

THE BEGINNING ERA

At the end of the Pre-Beginning, the Beginning Era started. According to the Scriptures, the heavens and the earth were made by God in the Beginning. The heavens and earth were not just empty spaces because, as a wise Being, God never made anything for uselessness or purposelessness. Everything has a purpose (Ecc.3:1).

"The Lord has made everything for its purpose"   (Pro.16:4 RSV)

"The Lord made everything for a purpose"   (Pro.16:4 CEB)

"The Lord has a reason for everything he does"   (Pro.16:4 CEV)

God created the heavens and the earth for a purpose, which is to bring pleasure to God (Rev.4:11).

Fig.2: The only thing we know with certainty that was there with God in the Pre-Beginning Era was *NOTHING*. At the end of the Pre-Beginning, the Beginning Era started. According to the Scriptures, the heavens and the earth were made by God in the Beginning.

Hart is a high school friend. He is very gifted in creative arts. He would draw virtually any interesting thing that he saw. Once he finished the drawing and painting, he would spend time savouring his drawings. This was in the early 1980s and internet and computers were not yet available for public use. If they were, Hart would have taken photos of his drawings and uploaded them onto the internet. The drawings were the works of his hands and he derived immense pleasure from them.

In the same way, God made the heavens and the earth for His pleasure. He savours immense pleasure from the works of His hands. Pleasure is another word for glory. That is, the heavens and the earth were created to bring glory to God.

Rome's Triumphant Procession – an Illustration of Glory

When Julius Caesar invaded Gaul, conquered and subdued the Gallic tribes in the decisive Battle of Alesia in 52 BC, in which a complete Roman victory resulted in the expansion of the Roman Republic over the whole of Gaul (mainly present-day France and Belgium), Caesar's fame spread ahead of him into his native country, Rome. As Caesar triumphantly entered into Rome, the Romans lined the streets to receive their illustrious son. The streets were decorated with Roman flags. First, a herald on horseback went ahead to announce the homecoming of Caesar, and this was followed by Caesar's military cantonment marching majestically with an air of pomposity amidst symphony of war drums and singing.

Next was the parade of the captured citizens of Gaul in chains as a tribute of Caesar's gallant soldiery. Then came in General Caesar himself, adorned with military attire and driven in a convoy of trained horse-trotting chariots, with roars of applause as he majestically rode towards the Capitoline Hill, where he would be received with honours by the Roman Senate.

That was the *Triumphant Procession*, often accorded to Rome's illustrious military generals. Thus, on successful conquest, the General would receive glory from Rome. To keep him humble and to remind him of his mortality during such glorious parades through the Roman streets, a man would be stationed directly behind the General to repeatedly and quietly utter the sublime words of antiquity in the General's ears: 'Remember, thou art mortal!'

Rome's Triumphant Procession is a vivid illustration of man's glory obtained from fellow man. The highest glory or pleasure is not obtained from immaterial objects or animals. A man derives the highest sense of pleasure when a fellow man acknowledges and recognises his work. God's ultimate glory would not come from just the immaterial elements of the heavens and earth, but from beings that have the life of God flowing through them. That is, the beings would be like God Himself. In other words, the heavens and the earth were made to be populated with God-like beings that would bring ultimate glory to God. That was the eternal purpose of creation.

> *"For Jehovah created the heavens and earth and put everything in place, and he made the world to be lived in, not to be an empty chaos. I am Jehovah, he says, and there is no other!"*
>
> *(Isa.45:18 TLB).*

CHAPTER 3

THE MORNING STARS – THE SONS OF GOD

STARTING FROM THE BEGINNING ERA, God made the heavens and the earth. They were not to be empty spaces, but to be filled by living creatures with the life of God that would bring ultimate glory or pleasure to the heart of divinity.

*"For Jehovah created the heavens and earth and put everything
in place, and he made the world to be lived in, not to be an empty
chaos. I am Jehovah, He says, and there is no other!"*

(Isa.45:18 TLB).

Thus, from the Beginning era, God made intelligent, moral beings to occupy and fill the heavens and the earth, and He set His Throne in the Third Heaven.

*"Where were you when I laid the foundation of the earth?
Tell Me, if you know and have understanding.
Who determined the measurements [of the earth], if you know?
Or who stretched the [measuring] line on it?
On what were its foundations fastened?
Or who laid its cornerstone,
When the morning stars sang together
And all the sons of God (angels) shouted for joy?"*

(Job 38:4-7 AMP)

In Job chapter 38 verses 4 to 7, God questioned Job on some salient matters about creation, revealing that He created beings, described as Morning Stars and Sons of God, right at the Beginning Era. These were beings that populated the earth and the heaven. They were the inhabitants of the worlds that God created.

The phrase 'morning stars' occurs three times in the scriptures: Job 38:7, Revelation 2:28 and Revelation 22:16. The phrase is taken from a compound Hebrew word *boqer kowkab*, which means, 'brightly shining numerous progeny or brethren.' The equivalent phrase in the New Testament Greek is *Proinos aster*.

'Morning stars' is often used interchangeably with 'sons of God,' and refer to beings that carry the life of God in them. In other words, God was letting Job know that before man's arrival on earth, there had been other beings that carried the life of God in them. These beings belong to a different race from humanity; that is, they are brethren of same stock, and they were numerous progeny of God; meaning that they were also of enormous population. They are the morning stars.

Thus, in the beginning when God created the Heaven and the Earth, He also created the 'morning stars' or 'sons of God,' who are beings carrying the life of God in them. Sonship designates origin. That is, a son originates from a father. The sons of God came from God; they have the life of God flowing through their beings. The Greek term for the 'life of God' is *zoe*. In other words, for a being to be called a son of God, he must have *zoe* running in his system.

The 'morning stars' mentioned in Job 38 versus 7 were the sons of God; they have zoe flowing in their system. These beings inhabited the heavens and the earth.

THE RACIAL CLASS OF THE MORNING STARS

Who were these morning stars? What race were they? Definitely, they were not of the human race; rather they were angelic. That is, these morning stars, who were sons of God, were angels.

Jude chapter 1 verse 13 was an interesting Scripture. It gave warning to rebellious, ungodly teachers.

"They [rebellious teachers] are like wandering stars forever doomed to the darkest pits of hell" (Jude 1:13 CEV).

Interestingly, Jude chapter 1 verse 13 likens the punishment that awaits these rebellious teachers to that of the fallen angels, who were also called 'wandering stars.' That is, these angels were morning stars until they fell out of favour with God to become wandering stars. This is discussed further in Chapter 11. Thus, these morning stars or sons of God were angelic beings (see also Job 1:6; 2:1). They inhabited the then earth.

CHAPTER 4
CATEGORIES OF MORNING STARS

THE MORNING STARS WERE CREATED at the Beginning Era to bring glory to God. They were the sons of God and were of the angelic race. One significant question will be: if all the morning stars were angels, are all angels morning stars? Studying the Bible, it becomes apparent that not all angels were privileged to be among the category of the morning stars.

> *"Where were you when I laid the foundation of the earth?*
> *When the morning stars sang together*
> *And all the sons of God (angels) shouted for joy?"*
>
> *(Job 38:4,7 AMP)*

Job chapter 38 verse 7 mentions 'morning stars' separately from 'sons of God.' All angels are sons of God as they all carry the life of God, *zoe*, in their nature. Indeed, some Bible versions translate 'sons of God' in the above Scriptures as *angels*.

However, not all these angelic sons of God are Morning Stars. Hence, Job chapter 38 verse 7 designates Morning Stars from the general population of angelic sons of God. In other words, Morning Stars are part of 'all the sons of God,' though of a different kind. It is like a tribe such as the Eskimos among the human race. Morning Stars are a 'tribe' among the angelic Sons of God. As you study this book further, you will realise that the Morning Stars were a category of angels that populated the earth and had access to heaven, where the Throne of God resides.

THE FOUR CATEGORIES OF ANGELS

A study of angelic beings will give us more information about these morning stars. Angels are not all of the same kind and class. Each angel is a spiritual entity of God's creation. Angels do not marry and give birth (Mat.22:30). That is, angels do not have fathers and mothers as humans here on earth. Angels are spiritual beings (1Cor.15:44).

Here on earth, we do not know the exact number of angels that God has created. However, the Scriptures suggest that they are in millions, if not billions. In fact, from the Scriptures, it appears the number of angels is more than the population of humans (Rev.5:11).

The myriad of angels can be grouped into four major categories as follows:

(1) Cherubim

In about 1447 BC, Moses was called up to climb to the top of Mount Sinai, where he was alone with God for about 40 days (see SSB Book 4). There on the mountain, Moses had an unusual encounter with Divinity that would not only transform him but would also change the history of Israel's nationhood and, by extrapolation, the entire humanity. It was on the mountain that Moses received the Ten Commandments, which today have become incorporated into national constitutions and form the basis of human right policies across the world.

Interestingly, while on top of Mount Sinai, God opened the eyes of Moses to peep into Heaven. Moses saw a Tabernacle in Heaven. Then God instructed him to build an earthly tabernacle exactly as the one he saw in Heaven. God told Moses: *"Be sure that you make everything according to the pattern I have shown you here on the mountain"* (Exo.25:40 NLT).

To show the seriousness of constructing the earthly Tabernacle according to the pattern of Heaven's Tabernacle, God reiterated to Moses several times: *"Set up this Tabernacle according to the pattern you were shown on the mountain*" (Exo.26:30 NLT). Because the intricacies of the tabernacle were heavenly, the engineering team that would construct Moses' Tabernacle would need the enablement of Heaven to be able to construct Moses' Tabernacle to be exactly as the Heaven's Tabernacle that Moses saw. Therefore, God called out men and filled them with His Spirit for artistic design and construction.

> *"So Bezalel, Oholiab and every skilled person to whom the Lord has given skill and ability to know how to carry out all the work of constructing the sanctuary are to do the work just as the Lord has commanded" (Exod.36:1 NIV).*

Later in Israel's history, King Solomon built a Temple in Jerusalem; he laid the foundation in 967 BC and finished construction in 960 BC (see SSB Book 4). Interestingly, the basic layout plan of this Temple was patterned after Moses' Tabernacle. When Solomon's Temple, also known as the First Temple, was destroyed by King Nebuchadnezzar in 586 BC, the returned Jewish exiles led by Zerubbabel laid the foundation of the Second Temple in 536 BC, and it was completed about 20 years later in 515 BC (Ezr.6:1-18; see SSB Book 4). The interesting thing about the Second Temple was that it was patterned after the First Temple, which was patterned after Moses' Tabernacle, which in turn was patterned after the Heavenly Tabernacle. In other words, there is a Tabernacle in Heaven.

The basic structure of the Mosaic Tabernacle, and hence the First and Second Temples, consisted of three parts: (a) the Outer Court, where the Jewish proselytes (Gentiles who were converted to Judaism) could stay to be part of some of the Jewish ritual ceremonies; (b) Holy Place, where only Jews could come into to participate in the ritual ceremonies; (c) the Holy of Holies, which was the most sacred place in Israel, and it was where only the High Priest could enter once in each year to carry out the solemn Atonement Rite for the sins of the Jewish nation (see SSB Book 4).

A further study of the Mosaic Tabernacle shows the sacred functions of a group of angels referred to as Cherubim (or Cherub, for short).

(a) Guardian of the Throne of God

Images of Cherubim were embroidered into the curtains of the Mosaic Tabernacle and the curtains that separate the Holy of Holies from the Holy Place.

> "The Holy Tent should be made from ten curtains. These curtains must be made from fine linen and blue, purple, and red yarn. A skilled worker should sew pictures of Cherub angels with wings into the curtains... Use fine linen and make a special curtain for the inside of the Holy Tent. Use blue, purple, and red yarn and sew pictures of Cherub angels into the curtain" (Exo.26:1,31 ERV).

> "Then the skilled workers began making the Holy Tent. They made the ten curtains from fine linen and blue, purple, and red yarn. And they sewed pictures of Cherub angels with wings into the curtains" (Exo.36:8 ERV).

By engraving the images of Cherub in the curtains of the Mosaic Tabernacle, and especially into the curtains that separate the Holy of Holies from the rest of the world, it shows the protective, guardian function of this category of angels. In other words, Cherubim guard the most sacred place, the Holy of Holies. This is exactly what happens in Heaven; Cherubim guard the sacred Throne of God in Heaven. This is such an important function that had influenced on the destiny of humanity as discussed later in this book.

(b) Guardian of the Sacred Laws

Placed within the Holy of Holies of Mosaic Tabernacle was the Ark of the Covenant. The Ark carried the Presence of God among the Jews, depicting the divine covenant that set the Jews apart from any other human race. The Presence of God, represented by the Ark of the Covenant, among the Jews was signalled by two activities:

• The Shekinah Glory
Shekinah glory was the visible Presence of God that would appear as a white cloud on top of the Ark of the Covenant and would occasionally fill the entire Tabernacle like it was during the dedication of the First Temple (1Kin.8:10,11).

The Ark of Covenant was a box of acacia wood covered with pure gold (Exo.25:10-15). The lid or covering of the Ark of the Covenant was called the **Mercy Seat**, and was one piece of pure gold, 45 inches (114.30 centimetres) long, 27 inches (68.58 centimetres) wide and 27 inches (68.58 centimetres) high. The Shekinah glory would appear as white cloud on top of the Mercy Seat, and God would speak audibly to the High Priest from the cloud as the High Priest ministered there in the Holy of Holies before God.

• The Sacred Law
In the Ark and directly under the Mercy Seat, were the most sacred religious items of Judaism – the Ten Commandments – written upon two tablets of stone (1Kin.8:9). Also enclosed in the Ark were some preserved pieces of heavenly bread, Manna, and the budded Rod of Aaron (Heb.9:3,4).

At each end of the Mercy Seat were carved images of the Cherubim, made of pure 'beaten' gold. These Cherubim stretched forth their wings on high, so as to cover the Mercy Seat, their faces being turned inward toward the Mercy Seat. That is, God instructed Moses to carve pictures of two Cherubim having their wings clasping over the Ark of the Covenant on the Mercy Seat (Exo.25:18).

Thus, the carved images of the Cherubs were positioned in such a way that they provided covering and protection of the Mercy Seat and the contents of the Ark. The glory of God would appear as a thick white cloud on the Mercy Seat, and God would speak to the High Priest from this cloud of Shekinah glory between the two carved Cherubim.

"I will give you the Agreement. Put it into this Box [Ark of Covenant]. Then make a lid, the mercy-cover. Make it from pure gold. Make it 2 1/2 cubits long and 1 1/2 cubits wide. Then make two Cherub angels and put them on each end of the mercy-cover. Hammer gold to make these angels. Put one angel on one end of the mercy-cover, and put the other angel on the other end. Join the angels together with the mercy-cover to make one piece. The wings of these angels should spread up toward the sky. The angels should cover the Box with their wings and should face each other, looking toward the mercy-cover...When I meet with you, I will speak from between the Cherub angels on the mercy-cover that is on the Box of the Agreement. From that place, I will give all my commands to the Israelites" (Exo.25:16-20,22 ERV).

**Fig.3: Two Cherubim with their wings spread over
the Mercy Seat of the Ark of the Covenant.**

Therefore, symbolically, the carved Cherubs guarded the Ten Commandments of God stored in the Ark. This was a replica of the chief function of the Cherub angels in Heaven. Again, let us not forget that the Tabernacle that Moses constructed was a replica of the Tabernacle in Heaven because God opened the eyes of Moses to peep into Heaven and thereafter constructed a Tabernacle after what he had seen (Exo.25:9,40). Hence, a review of the carved Cherubim of the Ark of the Covenant gives us more knowledge of the nature and functions of the Cherub angels. That is, the Cherub angels guard the Laws of God, the most sacred thing in Heaven and are before the Mercy Seat of God's Throne in Heaven.

(c) Guardian of the Words of God
The laws of God are the Words of God, which are perfect, eternal, and the most supreme of all:

> *"You have magnified Your word above all Your name"*
>
> *(Psa.138:2 NKJV).*

> *"For all the law is fulfilled in one word" (Gal.5:14 KJV).*

The Cherub angels guard the Words of God, ensuring their fulfilment. An example of this function of Cherubim was the incidence that occurred at the Fall of Man in about 4100 BC (see SSB Book 4). After delivering divine judgment and banishing man out of his home, the Garden of Eden, God stationed Cherub angels at the eastward of Eden to stop man from having access to the Tree of Life.

> *"So the Lord God banished them [Adam and Eve] from the Garden of Eden, and he sent Adam out to cultivate the ground from which he had been made. After sending them out, the Lord God stationed mighty cherubim to the east of the Garden of Eden. And he placed a flaming sword that flashed back and forth to guard the way to the tree of life" (Gen.3:23,24 NLT).*

In other words, God wanted the fallen man not to eat of the fruit of the Tree of Life and live forever in sin, thereby antagonising the very laws of God for humanity. To actualise that, God despatched Cherub angels to prevent Adam and Eve from accessing the fruit of the Tree of Life. That is, here again, Cherubim are also seen to guard the words of God, which are the laws of God and the very essence of divinity. The Cherubs literally blocked Adam and Eve from having access to the fruit of the Tree of Life, thus, enforcing divine verdict.

Fig.4: Cherubim are real beings, and they are the guardians of the sacred things of God.

The Most Fundamental Job in Heaven

A constitution is the most significant piece of identity of a people. A constitution defines a group of people, giving them a peculiarity and identity. A constitution is what gives birth to a nation, state, system, or government. The eternal laws of God are the Constitution of Heaven that orchestrate perfection in Heaven.

"The law of the Lord is perfect" (Psa.19:7 KJV).

The Laws of God formed the Foundation of the Throne of God. Thus, protecting divine laws is one of the most fundamental jobs to be entrusted to a creature. Cherubim are the custodians of these laws. That is, the Cherubim are among the privileged few angels that have direct access to the Throne of God and are endowed with the privileged function of guarding God's sacred laws.

In summary
In summary, therefore, the Cherubim are the guardians of the sacred things of God. To portray the significance of this function, the Bible records that:
- God dwells between Cherubs (1Sam.4:4; 2Sam.6:2)
- God speaks from the Mercy Seat between the Cherubs (Num.7:89)
- God rides upon the Cherubs (Psa.18:10).

Cherubim are known for their power and beauty (Gen.3:24; Eze.1:5-28; 28:12,13,17; 8:1-4; 10:1-22). Indeed, the significance of Cherubs in divinity is unquestionable.

(2) Seraphim

Seraphim is another class of angels, mentioned in the book of Isaiah chapter one. The word 'seraphim' (short form, seraph) literally means 'fiery ones' and probably stems from the fiery imagery often associated with the Presence of God (cf. Ezek. 1:27).

In about 740 BC, Prophet Isaiah had a vision of Heaven in which he saw Seraphim praising God. He saw each Seraph angel had three pairs of wings – one pair to cover his face so as not to gaze at the holiness of God's Presence, the other pair to cover his feet, apparently because of the sacredness of God's Presence, and the last pair to fly about in praises.

"In the year that King Uzziah died, I saw the Lord seated on a high and lofty throne, and His robe filled the temple. Seraphim were standing above Him; each one had six wings: with two he covered

his face, with two he covered his feet, and with two he flew. And one called to another: 'Holy, holy, holy is the Lord of Hosts; His glory fills the whole earth.' The foundations of the doorways shook at the sound of their voices, and the temple was filled with smoke" (Isaiah 6: 1-4 HCSB).

In other words, Seraphim have the principal function of rendering continuous praises to God. They are mighty angels that offer intense, fiery praises and worship unto our God. In addition, they can perform the duty of sin purification.

"Then one of the seraphim flew to me, having in his hand a burning coal that he had taken with tongs from the altar. And he touched my mouth and said: 'Behold, this has touched your lips; your guilt is taken away, and your sin atoned for'" (Isa.6:6,7 ESV).

Possibly, the four beasts saw by Apostle John in about AD 100 during his vision of Heaven were Seraphim. John described each of these angelic creatures as having six wings just as Prophet Isaiah had described in about 740 BC and that the angelic creatures stood in the Presence of God before the Eternal Throne in continuous worship of the Almighty (Rev.4:6-11).

These four angelic creatures seen by Apostle John during his vision of Heaven in about AD 100 were not the same angelic creatures that Prophet Ezekiel saw by the Chebar River at Babylon in about 592 BC. Prophet Ezekiel saw four living creatures, each with four wings, and he identified them as Cherub angels (Eze. chpt.1 and 10). That is, both the Cherubim and the Seraphim are privileged angels that stand in the Presence of God before the Eternal Throne.

Fig.5: A Seraph angel with six wings as seen by Prophet Isaiah in about 740 BC.

(3) Missive angels

It appears this group forms the bulk of the population of angels. Missive angels have the function of communicating divine messages. They take the divine messages from God across the world. It appears the Morning Stars are primarily missive angels saddled with the responsibility of establishing divine program and agenda on earth. They have access to Heaven, where the Throne of God resides, and are meant to communicate and perpetuate Heaven's lifestyle on earth.

Later, when man appeared, missive angels were busy communicating divine messages from Heaven to earth. A good example was the experience of Jacob son of Isaac. Jacob was fleeing from his brother Esau in about 1967 BC after a family altercation. He arrived at Bethel, which was about 640 kilometres from Haran, where his uncle, Laban lived. With the darkness of the night overshadowing him, he decided to rest right there in the bush, using a stone as his pillow. While sleeping that night, he had a dream.

"Now Jacob left Beersheba [never to see his mother again] and travelled toward Haran. And he came to a certain place and stayed overnight there because the sun had set. Taking one of the stones of the place, he put it under his head and lay down there [to sleep]. He dreamed that there was a ladder (stairway) placed on the earth, and the top of it reached [out of sight] toward heaven; and [he saw] the angels of God ascending and descending on it [going to and from heaven]" (Gen.28:10-12 AMP).

The angels ascending and descending the ladder where the missive angels bearing the divine messages from Heaven to earth. Never doubt this truth, there are large numbers of angels that are busy on earth today communicating divine agenda!

Fig.6: Never doubt this truth, there are large numbers of angels that are busy on earth today communicating divine agenda!

(4) Combative Angels

About 20 years after his encounter at Bethel, Jacob again met an angel of the Lord in the night. It was an encounter that would eternally impact positively on his destiny. Jacob had a gruelling combat with this angel all through that night into the early hours of the morning. Whether the combat was a physical wrestling or a spiritual contest, that is subject to one's interpretation. All we know was that by the end of the combat, by divine enablement, the combative angel changed the name Jacob (from Hebrew word *Ya`aqob*, which means 'a supplanter') to Israel, which is from the Hebrew word *Yisra'el* that means 'prevailer' or 'a prince' (Gen.32:28).

Aside from the missive angels, combative angels appear to be about the most numerous of all the categories of angels. In fact, the Bible addresses God Himself in connection with the combative angels. The Scriptures often address God as the Lord of Hosts (1Sam.1:3; 1Chr.17:7; Psa.80:4). The term 'host' is from the Hebrew word *tsaba*, which literally means 'war, warfare, battle, or army.' It refers to a combat of angelic battalion that are sent forth to execute divine command.

In about 845 BC, during the reign of King Jehoram of the Northern Kingdom of Israel, the King of Syria, Hadadezer, dispatched a regiment of soldiers to arrest Prophet Elisha for using his prophetic gifts to forestall Syria's threat against the Northern Kingdom of Israel. The servant of Prophet Elisha woke up at night to see these foreign soldiers around their house. Panic set in and with such trepidations, he woke up the Prophet. But the Prophet was conscious of the hosts of angelic combat about them. All he did was to pray:

"Lord, I pray, open his eyes that he may see" (2Kin.6:17 NKJV).

When his spiritual eyes were opened, Elisha's servant was stunned to see a large host of combative angels guarding them (2Kin.6:8-23).

In addition, during the arrest of Jesus at the Garden of Gethsemane in AD 33 by the combined Jewish authorities, the initial reaction of Jesus' disciples was to fight back. However, Jesus countered the disciples' feeble effort with this revealing statement:

"Do you think that I cannot call on My Father, and He will provide Me at once with more than 12 legions of angels?"

(Mat.26:53 HCSB).

A legion is a Latin word for military conscription and it was the largest unit of the Roman army, consisting of about 6000 soldiers. In other words, about 72000 combative angels could be mobilised at once just at a behest call of Jesus! It leaves us to imagine how many combative angels are there in total! Possibly in billions!

Fig.7: It appears the Morning Stars are primarily missive angels saddled with the responsibility of establishing divine program and agenda on earth. They have access to Heaven, where the Throne of God resides, and are meant to communicate and perpetuate Heaven's lifestyle on earth.

Guardian Angels

Due to their protective function towards God's people, some refer to combative angels as **Guardian Angels**. Guardian angels are the angels that guard and guide God's people (Psa.91:12) and little children (Mat.18:10). They guard and guide people by protecting them (2Kin.6:14-17), directing them in life, and ministering help by strengthening them. For instance, guardian angels were fully part of the earthly Ministry of Jesus on earth (Mat.4:11), strengthened Him in time of trials (Luk.22:39-43), and even rolled away the stone at Jesus' tomb after His resurrection (Mat.28:1-3).

Guardian angels have been very active since the birth of the Church in AD 33. They guard and guide believers. For instance, they protected and delivered the believers from King Herod's prison (Act.5:17-20; 12:6-10), they protected Apostle Paul and all other passengers with him on a ship voyage to Rome (Act.27:21-26). They play active role in evangelism of the world with the Gospel, hence, they are often referred to as **Reaper Angels**. For example, a guardian angel directed Evangelist Philip to preach to an Ethiopian eunuch, the Treasurer of Candace, Queen of the Ethiopians (Act.8:26), and according to Church history, it was by this encounter Ethiopia and some parts of Africa were evangelised (see SSB Book 4).

A guardian angel directed the conversion of Cornelius, the Roman soldier, and his household through the ministry of Apostle Peter (Acts chapter 10). A guardian angel also gave divine direction for Apostle Paul's ministry to Europe via Macedonia (Act.16:9,10). In fact, the end-time massive world evangelism with the Gospel by the Church will not be possible or effective without the activities of these Reaper Angels (Mat.13:30,39).

CHAPTER 5

THE ARCHANGELS

As DISCUSSED IN CHAPTER 4, there are basically four classes or categories of angels – cherubim, seraphim, missive and combative. Interestingly, no matter the class, angels are not of the same rank and title. The archangelic group refers to angels that are principal or chief in rank. In other words, the archangels are the leaders among the angelic categories.

CHARACTERISTICS OF ARCHANGELS

Archangels have the following three characteristics:

(a) Direct Access
Not all angels can have direct access to the Presence of God. However, archangels are generally privileged to have direct access to the Presence of God as they stand before Him in ministration.

(b) Specific Assignment
Each archangel is in charge of a specific assignment.

(c) Assigned Authority
The Kingdom of God is a well-organised system with specified delegated authorities and functions. Each archangel is a commander of divine order. That is, each archangel can mobilise other angels to execute the commands of God. An archangel is a chief or a principal angel. In other words, each archangel has a specific office with

many other angels under his command. Hence, an archangel wields enormous influence over other angels.

Some archangels have control over assigned territories in which they exercise their authorities, hence, they are also called Chief Princes (see Dan.10:13). That is, archangels have controlling power over regions with many other angels under their control.

FOUR KNOWN ARCHANGELS

Four angels have been identified as archangels in the Scriptures; there may be more that are not specifically mentioned in the Bible:

(1) MICHAEL

Michael is the archangel in charge of fighting off opposition against divine agenda. He is Heaven's Minister of Defence. Michael is the archangel in charge of war and he can mobilise other angels to wage war against opposition. Apparently, he is the Head of the Combative Angels.

> *"There was war in heaven: Michael and his angels fought the dragon. The dragon and his angels fought back" (Rev.12:7 CEB).*

In another instance, it was Archangel Michael who fought the demonic Principal over Persia that blocked answers to Daniel's prayers in about 600 BC (Daniel chapter 10).

In about 2068 BC, Abraham had a divine visitation. The Lord Himself with two combative angels visited Abraham's household to enforce the divine program of the birth of Isaac (Genesis chapter 18). Later the Lord went up to Heaven but the two combative angels journeyed down to Sodom and Gomorrah, the neighbouring cities that were rife with immorality and vices of all kinds, especially homosexuality. By the enablement of these two combative angels,

Abraham's nephew, Lot with his household, was delivered while divine judgment of fire and brimstone came upon the adulterous cities (Genesis chapter 19).

Most likely one of the two combative angels that visited Abraham and later brought judgment upon Sodom and Gomorrah was the Archangel Michael. In addition, possibly, it was the Archangel Michael that appeared twice to Abraham's concubine, Hagar (Gen. chpt.16 and 21). Also, it was most likely the Archangel Michael that appeared to Abraham when he was about to sacrifice his son, Isaac, during the time God tested him (Gen. chpt.22). Interestingly, Abraham was very conscious of the presence of this archangel around him and his household. When it was time to pick a wife for his son, Isaac, Abraham acknowledged that the angel would guide his servant to choose the correct woman for Isaac:

> *"But Abraham said to him, Beware that you do not take my son back there. The Lord God of heaven, who took me from my father's house and from the land of my family, and who spoke to me and swore to me, saying, 'To your descendants I give this land,' He will send His angel before you, and you shall take a wife for my son from there" (Gen.24:6,7 NKJV).*

Possibly, it was this same Archangel Michael that appeared to Jacob in Mesopotamia (Gen.31:11-13). Indeed, the combative angel that wrestled with Jacob, an event that changed Jacob's destiny, seems to be the Archangel Michael (Gen.32:24-32).

The Angel of His Presence

Jacob, the grandson of Abraham, through his twelve sons would lay the foundation of the formation of the nation of Israel. In about 1877 BC, Jacob moved into Egypt with 70 members of his household to join his son, Joseph, who was promoted by divine enablement to the exalted position of a Prime Minister of the most powerful nation in the then world (Gen. chpt. 46). While blessing Joseph and Joseph's children, Jacob acknowledged the presence of the same Angel that guarded his father Isaac, and his grandfather, Abraham, in his life. Jacob also mentioned that this same Angel would guide and guard Joseph's children, Ephraim and Manasseh, until they would grow to form nationhood with the rest of his other children.

> *"And he blessed Joseph, and said:*
> *'God, before whom my fathers Abraham and Isaac walked,*
> *The God who has fed me all my life long to this day,*
> *The Angel who has redeemed me from all evil,*
> *Bless the lads;*
> *Let my name be named upon them,*
> *And the name of my fathers Abraham and Isaac;*
> *And let them grow into a multitude in the midst of the earth'"*
> *(Gen.48:15,16 NKJV).*

In Egypt, Jacob's household soon grew into formidable twelve tribes that alarmed the Egyptians, who forcefully conscripted them to be slaves. Nonetheless, the Angel that God assigned to Abraham, Isaac, and Jacob, was with the twelve tribes as they grew into the nation of Israel.

Later in about 1447 BC, Moses was called to deliver the twelve tribes from the Egyptian bondage. The remarkable call of Moses to the ministry of delivering the Israelites from the bondages of the Egyptians started with the appearance of the Angel of the Lord in a blazing flame of fire from the midst of a bush; the bush was on fire, yet it was not consumed. That caught the attention of Moses, who turned to have a closer look. As he did so, the Lord God appeared to Him (Exod. chapter 3). In other words, the Lord first sent His Angel to draw Moses' attention before He then appeared to Moses.

Later, it was this Angel that God used to lead Israel out of Egypt (Exod.14:19) and finally brought them into the Promised Land (Exo.23:20-23; 32:34; 33:2). This Angel was later identified by Prophet Isaiah as the *Angel of His (God's) Presence*, also known as *Angel of His Face*.

"In all their affliction He was afflicted,
And the Angel of His Presence saved them;
In His love and in His pity He redeemed them;
And He bore them and carried them
All the days of old" (Isa.63:9 NKJV).

Some theologians argue that the Angel of His Presence refers to the Lord God Himself. However, there is no Biblical evidence of this. Obviously, the Angel of His Presence is the archangel God assigns to guard and direct Israel as a nation from the Egyptian enslavement into the Promised Land. He must be a mighty angel with several other angels under his command, an archangel who have direct access to the Presence of the Almighty God. Who could this Archangel be?

The Angelic Prince of Israel

The non-canonical Second Book of Enoch identifies four archangels as having direct access to the Presence of God, and these four archangels are Michael, Gabriel, Uriel, and Raphael. The last two names are not mentioned in the 66 canonized books of the Bible. Which Archangel could have been referred to as the Angel of His Presence that God used to deliver Israel from Egypt?

Obviously, he should be Archangel Michael. As stated above, archangels have control over assigned territories in which they exercise their authorities, and Archangel Michael is the angelic Prince that God has assigned over the nation of Israel (Dan.10:13,21; 12:1).

"Michael, the mighty angelic prince who stands guard over your
nation [Israel]" (Dan.12:1 TLB).

In other words, it was the Archangel Michael that God assigned to Abraham; the archangel guarded Abraham along with all people and everything connected to Abraham, and later he was with Isaac, Jacob and through generations until Jacob's descendants grew into the nation of Israel. Michael was the Angel of His Presence that God used to deliver the Israelites from Egypt. As a nation, God still assigns Archangel Michael to oversee the welfare of Israel; he is the angelic Prince of Israel.

Significant Lesson for Us All

Notice this important trend: an angel was assigned by God to Abraham. This angel worked with/for Abraham down through Abraham's generations unto the time his descendants became the nation of Israel. The significant lesson here is that God does assign an angel to His child, and the assigned angel works with/for the individual, transports him to Heaven when his earthly journey ends, and then the assigned angel continues to work with/for the individual's family that are still on earth throughout generations.

Personal Testimony of Angelic Presence

As clearly stated in the Scriptures, every child of God has a guardian angel (Mat.18:10; Heb.1:13,14), and many children of God do come in direct contact with the ministry of guardian angels in their lives; a lot of such testimonies abound. Personally, I am very conscious of the angelic presence around me and my household. The following story is a testimony of the ministry of the guardian angel God has assigned unto me and my household.

At about 12 midnight on 18th December 1995, I left the University of Port Harcourt Teaching Hospital (UPTH) for the campus of the Rivers State University of Science and Technology (RSUST) after a student hospital call. I was in the clinical class of the medical school, and as part of the training programmes, we rotated through units in the hospital. The old site of the hospital was in the centre of the town, few kilometres from RSUST campus, where my junior brother was an Accounting student. I had planned to pass the night in his hostel room, so I boarded a bus going that way.

Shortly after boarding the bus, I heard a voice, which said: 'This man (referring to the driver) is taking you to nowhere but to their shrine for sacrifices.' Of course, I knew it was the voice of the Spirit of God, revealing the secret plan of the driver. The driver was taking me for their occultic money rituals! The message was so clear and loud in my heart that I thought the driver heard it. Subsequent events, however, suggested he did not. Rather the Spirit of God spoke authoritatively into my spirit man, and I picked up the message.

At this time in Nigeria, there was this increased incidence of occult practices with cannibalistic rituals. Around that time, Ndidi, a schoolmate and a member of our campus fellowship, was kidnapped by ritual killers. If not for the prayers of the Church, she would have been sacrificed for rituals like some others who were also abducted with her. She escaped miraculously.

That night I was alone in the bus with the driver. When I heard that message from the Spirit of God, I started roving my eyes about to locate the possible places the driver might have hid any weapon, because we had heard that ritual killers usually first handcuff, blindfold and mouth-gag their victims. My plan was to lunge at such weapons, confiscate them, and throw them away; thereafter seize the steering of the bus while still on motion with the aim of overpowering the driver and then escape out of the vehicle.

I quickly appraised the driver. He looked like a middle-aged man, possibly mid-forties, with central alopecia and trimmed side-facial hairs. I was sitting at the right side of the vehicle, just a seat behind the driver. While contemplating my course of actions, God did something that changed my perception of the spiritual world!

From nowhere, a man suddenly appeared in the vehicle! He was about 5.6 feet in height, dressed in clothes that looked rumbled. By my estimation, he looked like someone in his mid-30s. He appeared a few steps behind me, holding some piece of stick in his right hand above his head and a sac that hanged over the left shoulder but held at the end with the left hand. The man began to advance forward. On hearing the footsteps of this stranger, the driver reflexively turned backwards and there saw the man approaching him. With an air of anger, the stranger took some steps towards the driver, holding the stick over the driver's head as if he was about to hit him with it.

Meanwhile, some boldness was welling up in me; the boldness was not because I saw another person in the bus. Rather it was an inward boldness of faith that came upon me with no fear whatsoever. With such boldness in me, I quickly assessed the stranger. He didn't talk or make any further movement, but just stood right behind the driver as if he was ready to hit his head with the stick. The driver, apparently out of fear, quickly stopped the vehicle right in the middle of the road; thank God there was no traffic at that time of the day. By my assessment, the contents of the sac the stranger carried were like some pieces of stones.

From all indications, the stranger appeared for my rescue. Apparently, he was ready to attack the driver if he continued on his evil mission. Thus, with a quivering voice, the driver addressed me: 'Please, Sir, kindly come down.'

I did not leave the vehicle immediately. Still filled with boldness, I took a last look at the driver and the stranger, opened the door, got off, and moved to the pedestrian roadside. When he was certain that I was out of the vehicle, the stranger left the bus and came down after me, moved to the roadside and started walking in the direction we came. I stood still, watching the stranger, who moved few steps, and all of a sudden vanished! He just disappeared right before my eyes. I blinked my eyes several times to be sure I was seeing correctly. There was no sight of the stranger any more. It then dawned on me that I just had a divine rescue from ritual killers! Meanwhile, the driver started his engine and drove off.

I saw a motorcyclist, who picked me up. Excited about the divine rescue, I started sharing my testimony right there with the cyclist. On hearing my testimony, the cyclist was alarmed. He quickly dropped me by the roadside and took off in fright. Shortly, I saw another cyclist who drove me to the RSUST, where I learnt my brother had travelled out of campus. With so much excitement, I shared my testimony that same night with the available students, and everybody was excited about the divine rescue. The next Sunday, I was right in Glorious Covenant Church, where I worshipped, to share my testimony of rescue from ritual killers by the mercy of God!

Obviously, the stranger that appeared in that bus was my guidance angel, who dressed in rugged attires to frighten and possibly hit the driver in order to frustrate his evil plan against me.

(2) ANGEL OF DEATH

The Angel of Death is popularly called the *Destroyer* by most Bible translations like KJV, NIV, and AMP while a few translations like CEV, CJB, EXB and GNT use the phrase Death Angel, Angel of Death or Slaughterer (see Exo.12:23). He is in charge of enforcing divine judgment of death against the condemned.

As mentioned above, one of the two combative angels that appeared to Abraham in about 2068 BC was Archangel Michael. Possibly, the second combative angel in that company that appeared to Abraham in Mamre of Canaan was the Angel of Death. It was, therefore, Archangel Michael and the Angel of Death that left Abraham and moved into Sodom and Gomorrah to execute divine judgment on the iniquity of these two cities while rescuing Abraham's nephew, Lot, and his family (Gen. chpt. 18 and 19).

The Angel of Death was the one that killed all the firstborns of Egypt in the fateful night of divine judgment.

> *"For Jehovah will pass through the land and kill the Egyptians; but when he sees the blood upon the panel at the top of the door and on the two side pieces, he will pass over that home and not permit the Destroyer to enter and kill your firstborn" (Exo.12:23 TLB).*

It was this same Angel of Death, the Destroyer, that meted out divine punishment on Israel on account of David's sin in late 970s BC.

"And God sent an angel to Jerusalem to destroy it; but as he was about to destroy it, the Lord saw and was sorry over the calamity, and said to the Destroying Angel, 'It is enough; now relax your hand.' And the angel of the Lord was standing by the threshing floor of Ornan the Jebusite. Then David lifted up his eyes and saw the angel of the Lord standing between earth and heaven, with his drawn sword in his hand stretched out over Jerusalem. Then David and the elders, covered with sackcloth, fell on their faces"
(1Chr.21:15,16 NASB).

"And God sent an angel to destroy Jerusalem. But just as the angel was preparing to destroy it, the Lord relented and said to the Death Angel, 'Stop! That is enough!' At that moment the angel of the Lord was standing by the threshing floor of Araunah the Jebusite. David looked up and saw the angel of the Lord standing between heaven and earth with his sword drawn, reaching out over Jerusalem. So David and the leaders of Israel put on burlap to show their deep distress and fell face down on the ground"
(1Chr.21:15,16 NLT).

The Angel of Death is obviously an archangel, possibly the leader of the cherub angels after the dethronement of Lucifer. The Angel of Death, apparently, has many other subordinate angels under his command. For instance, at the final judgment of God, the Angel of Death will lead his host of avenging angels to execute divine judgment against all oppositions.

"And now I saw a pale horse, and its rider's name was Death. And there followed after him another horse whose rider's name was Hell. They were given control of one-fourth of the earth, to kill with war and famine and disease and wild animals" (Rev.6:8 TLB).

The mighty death power of this archangel, the Angel of Death, can be seen in his operation. In one night of operation, he singlehandedly killed 185 000 soldiers in the Assyrian military camp in 701 BC.

"That same night the Lord sent an angel to the camp of the Assyrians, and he killed one hundred and eighty-five thousands of them. And so the next morning, the camp was full of dead bodies"
(2Kin.19:35 CEV).

(3) GABRIEL

Gabriel is the Archangel in charge of relaying divine messages. He is the Heaven's Minister of Information. Obviously, Archangel Gabriel is the leader of the missive angels. He can despatch other missive angels to convey divine command. However, when it comes to conveying significant information, he does that by himself.

For instance, it was Gabriel who relayed important world events such as the coming of the Messiah to Prophet Daniel in about 600 BC. About 600 years later, he was despatched by God to communicate the fulfilment of the promise, which started with the birth of the Messiah's forerunner, John the Baptist (Luk.1:1-25), and finally the birth of the Messiah, Jesus Christ (Luk.1:26-38).

As mentioned above, not all angels can have direct access to the Presence of God. However, Gabriel, being an archangel, does stand before God in ministration. For instance, Archangel Gabriel informed the Jewish High Priest Zachariah, father of John the Baptist in about 2 BC:

"I am Gabriel; I stand and minister in the [very] presence of God, and I have been sent [by Him] to speak to you and to bring you this good news" (Luk.1:19 AMP).

(4) LUCIFER

This is the fourth archangel identifies in the Scriptures, and he has such a unique history and a great impact on humanity that a closer study of this angelic personality is necessary. Lucifer is discussed in the next chapter.

In Summary

The books of the Bible are the progressive revelation of God and how He structures His creation. God created the angels many years (possibly millions of years) before the creation of man and assigned them roles. Table 1 give the Categories of Angels and their Archangelic Leaders.

Table 1: Categories of Angels and their Archangelic Leaders		
Category of Angels	**Function of Category**	**Archangelic Leader**
Cherub angels	The guardians of the sacred things of God	*Lucifer
Seraph angels	Continuous worship of the Almighty	Angel of His Presence
Combative angels	Constitute the military Host of Heaven	**Michael
Missive angels	Communicate divine messages	Gabriel

*Lucifer was the archangelic leader of the Cherub angels, but he was dethroned following his rebellion.
**Before the entrance of sin into creation, it appears Combative Angels were part of the Seraph Angels. However, following the appearance of sin, Combative Angelic unit was formed from the Seraphim with the function of executing justice where necessary. Michael, one of the Angels of His Presence, was assigned the archangelic leadership of the formed Combative Angelic unit; the archangelic leadership function of Seraphim would have been assigned to some other archangel, either Uriel or Raphael as suggested by the non-canonical Book of Enoch.

THROUGHOUT HUMAN HISTORY, MAN HAS been fascinated by the nature of Lucifer. Was he real or a mere mystical personality? Interestingly, Lucifer is a real personality.

AN UNUSUAL GUEST ON UNIVERSITY CAMPUS

While I was a varsity student in the medical school, on a certain day we had an unusual guest, Mr. Karim, in our Christian campus fellowship.

Karim had a crave for power right from early childhood. Soon he became initiated into a secret cult. That action marked a journey of spiritual experience into the world of occultism. His fervent zeal soon made him to rise in rank in spiritism to the point that he became an occult master.

During those 30 years in occultism, Karim came in contact with the once-named angel Lucifer, who was his lord and master. Karim communed with Lucifer and carried out his assigned evil deeds. Later Karim came in contact with the power of God in Christ Jesus that regenerated him through the New Birth (the Born Again) experience. That was the reason he came to our Christian campus fellowship on invitation for his testimony.

In other words, like archangels Gabriel and Michael, who are real personalities and are still active in service of God today, the same manner Lucifer was a real personality and still active in his evil deeds.

THE SEVEN CHARACTERISTICS OF LUCIFER

Lucifer has been an angel of great interest and intrigues to humans. The characteristic nature of this angelic being is worth closer attention, and below is the seven characteristics of his nature.

First Characteristic: Lucifer was a Morning Star

Lucifer was one of the angelic sons of God. As stated above, one characteristic of sons of God is that they have the life of God or *zoe* in their nature. Morning Stars are a class of sons of God (Job 38:4-7). Lucifer was a morning star, one of the sons of God with *zoe*, the very life of God, flowing through him.

"...Lucifer, son of the morning!" (Isa.14:12 KJV)

"...morning star, son of the dawn!" (Isa.14:12 NIV)

Lucifer is from the Hebrew word *heylel*, which translates as 'shining one, light-bearer, or the morning star.' Lucifer was mentioned in Isaiah chapter 14 as the king of Babylon, and in the Jewish and Church history, the chapter is generally believed to refer to an angelic personality, a spirit who possessed and used the rulers of Babylon for his wicked acts, hence, the spirit is referred to as the king of Babylon. The title 'King of Babylon' in Isaiah chapter 14 was a metaphor for this angelic personality. A study of the chapter attests to this; for example, verse 13 records:

"You said to yourself, 'I'll climb to heaven and place my throne above the highest stars. I'll sit there with the gods far away in the north. I'll be above the clouds, just like God Most High'"
(Isa.14:13,14 CEV).

The above statement (Isa.14:13,14) were the words of Lucifer. Such a boastful attempt could not be from a human, but from an angelic entity, who had been with God and had access to Heaven. Here,

Lucifer boasted he would climb to heaven, which according to the Scriptures is located northwards (Psa.48:1,2), and place his throne above the Throne of God and rule there with his subordinates, whom he called 'gods.'

Second Characteristic: Lucifer was a Creature of God

Note that Lucifer was created by God; Lucifer himself was not the Creator. God created the angel Lucifer. He was created perfect in nature and physical beauty.

> *"You were perfect in your ways from the day you were created..."*
> *(Eze.28:15 NKJV)*

Ezekiel chapter 28 from verse 11 describes Lucifer. Note Ezekiel 28 verses 1 to 10 refers to the Prince of Tyre, a human being, but from verse 11 to 19 it refers to the King of Tyre, who was found in the Garden of Eden. The only humans found in the Garden were Adam and Eve; no human after the Fall was allowed into the Garden because God placed a Cherub angel to stop human from venturing into the Garden. Hence, Ezekiel 28 from verse 11 was referring not to a human being but an angelic being who was in the Garden of Eden.

The angelic being known in that Garden was Satan, previously known as Lucifer. Subsequent verses of Ezekiel chapter 28 give a vivid description of this angelic personality. Indeed, such descriptions as Ezekiel chapter 28 are generally believed by teachers and students of the Bible to refer to the angel Lucifer. The title 'King of Tyre' depicted the unsolicited, ignoble rule of Satan over Tyre territory.

Ezekiel chapter 28 verse 15 emphatically confirmed that Lucifer was created and he was not a 'creator' as some people erroneously believe. Lucifer was a Cherub angel created by God. The term 'create' is from the Hebrew word *'bara,'* which means 'to produce something from non-existing material substance.' It is the same words used for the creation of the human spirit. In other words, like the human spirit, Lucifer was created a spirit being, an angelic being.

Third Characteristic: Lucifer's body was formed from precious stones

Ezekiel chapter 28 indicates that Lucifer had a physical body. Indeed, all the morning stars that inhabited the earth had physical bodies. Without a physical body no being can legally operate on earth. This is the *Law of Terrestrial Existence*, which states that any organism that must inhabit the earth legally must have a physical body that comes from the earth. A physical or terrestrial body gives legal existence to the organism on earth (see SSB Book 1). Thus, Lucifer and all other morning stars that dwelt on earth had physical bodies that accorded them the legal right to dwell and do business on earth.

> *"Thus says the Lord God:*
> *'You were the seal of perfection,*
> *Full of wisdom and perfect in beauty.*
> *You were in Eden, the garden of God;*
> *Every precious stone was your covering:*
> *The sardius, topaz, and diamond,*
> *Beryl, onyx, and jasper,*
> *Sapphire, turquoise, and emerald with gold'"*
>
> *(Eze.28:12,13a NKJV)*

The term 'covering' in the above Scripture is from the Hebrew word *mĕcukkah*, which refers to physical covering, body or garniture. It actually refers to the physical body of Lucifer, one of the morning stars. However, Lucifer's body, unlike human body that was formed from the dust of the earth, was formed from precious stones. He was an embodiment of perfect, exquisite beauty to behold.

Fourth Characteristic: Lucifer had an Ecstatic Body for Music

The physical and spiritual built of Lucifer was constructed to produce ecstatic, sonorous tunes of music.

> *"The workmanship of your timbrels and pipes*
> *Was prepared for you on the day you were created'"*
>
> *(Eze.28:13b NKJV).*

The timbrels and pipes were instruments of music. Music is an integral aspect of the worship of God; all through the Scriptures, worship of God is often filled with songs and melody. Obviously, one of the functions of Lucifer was the coordination of God's worship on Earth as it is in Heaven. He was a great Choir Master, unrivalled in history. Lucifer was a beautiful creature, indeed, with a beautiful voice and body make-up for worship! The Creator specifically crafted Lucifer for worship that would bring glory or pleasure to the heart of divinity. Indeed, Lucifer was perfectly designed for grandiose worship of the Most High God.

Fifth Characteristic: Lucifer was Full of Wisdom

Not only was Lucifer created by God in perfect beauty, but he was also filled with wisdom. He radiated surpassing wisdom that was endowed on him by his Creator, Jehovah God. It was an unparalleled wisdom meant to bring God glory among the whole realm of creation.

> *"Thus says the Lord God:*
> *'You were the seal of perfection,*
> *Full of wisdom and perfect in beauty'" (Eze.28:12 NKJV)*

When he appeared in the Garden of Eden years later as the Serpent (by then he had lost all forms of civility due to divine judgment as discussed in the next chapter), Lucifer was described as the most subtle of any wild creature. That subtlety was the remnant and a tale of the great wisdom he possessed before his fall.

"Now the serpent was more subtle than any other wild creature that the Lord God had made" (Gen.3:1 RSV)

Sixth Characteristic: Lucifer was a Cherub Angel
Lucifer was created an angel. He was created a Cherub angel.

"You were the anointed cherub..." (Eze.28:14a NKJV)

As stated above, Cherubs are angels entrusted with guarding the sacred things such as guarding the Laws of God. Lucifer was one of the angels entrusted with such divine responsibility. Thus, Lucifer was a Cherub angel that was privileged to have direct access to God's Throne.

Seventh Characteristic: Lucifer was the Anointed Cherub that 'Covereth'
Lucifer was a cherub angel of God with a difference. He was not just a cherub angel, but a 'covering cherub.'

"You were the anointed cherub who covers..." (Eze.28:14a NKJV)

The Hebrew word for 'cover' in the above Scripture is *cakak*, which means 'covering or defence,' and it describes the functional duty of Lucifer as the defender of Divine Constitution. As discussed in Chapter 4, protecting divine laws is one of the most fundamental jobs to be entrusted to a creature, because the Laws of God formed the Foundation of the Throne of God. The Laws of God are the constitution of existence and Cherubim are the custodians of these laws. As the Covering Cherub, Lucifer was the Chief of Staff of Divinity. He was saddled with the responsibility of protecting the divine constitution of existence.

A 'covering cherub' means he was a chief cherub, an archangel that provides leadership to others. Lucifer was the cherub archangel in the same archangelic category as Michael and Gabriel. In other words, he had authority over many other angels and directly in charge of protection of God's laws. Apparently, he was the Leader of all cherub angels, a post of great grandeur and influence.

Chapter 7

PRE-HUMAN POPULATION ON EARTH

THE EARTH AND HEAVEN COULD not just be empty as God designed them for habitation (Isa.45:18). What many people do not realise was that the Morning Stars inhabited planet earth. Thus, before the tainting of the divine order of perfection with sin, these Morning Stars constituted part of the sons of God that have *zoe*, the life of God, flowing through them. The Morning Stars were of an angelic race. In other words, at the beginning of creation, some of the angels constituted the Morning Stars and lived on earth. Their original function was to fill the earth with the glory of God as it is in Heaven (Rev.4:11).

ANCIENT DWELLERS ON EARTH

Did the Morning Stars that dwelt on earth have physical bodies? What was the population of these morning stars that inhabited the earth?

Scriptural study shows that those Morning Stars that inhabited the earth had physical bodies.

> *"I turned you to ashes upon the earth in the sight of all who saw you. All who knew you among the peoples are astonished at you ..." (Eze.28:18,19a NKJV).*

The above Scripture (Eze.28:18,19a) refers to Lucifer, one of the morning stars on earth. The Scripture shows that during the divine judgment of Lucifer (discussed in Chapter 10), all the fellow dwellers, 'the peoples,' on earth with Lucifer were astonished at how he had been disgraced and debased. In other words, Morning Stars inhabited the earth, however, we do not know their exact number. Their population must have been in millions of millions (especially considering such huge population of angels that Apostle John saw in Heaven – Rev.5:11).

Thus, these morning stars were real people that set up divisions (countries, in modern language) on earth. They filled the earth, setting out nations and statutes. In other words, they were people with physical bodies and they formed nations on earth. This is in consonance with the *Law of Terrestrial Existence*, which states that only beings with physical bodies can exist and function legally in the physical world (see SSB Book 1).

These morning stars carried out activities that included merchandise on earth and it was obvious that the earth was full of these beings.

> *"You traded with other nations and became more and more cruel and evil. So I forced you to leave my mountain, and the creature that had been your protector now chased you away from the gems" (Eze.28:16).*

The above Scripture also refers to Lucifer and the other Morning Stars. They set up nations on earth that traded among each other. There were plants and various animals on earth then. In other words, the then earth was not different from the present earth. Indeed, it appears these Morning Stars made some appreciable progress in civilisation in their time.

THE PRINCE OF THE EARTH

As stated in the previous chapter, Lucifer was not just a Morning Star but the Chief Morning Star; that is, he was the Chief of all the Morning Stars that dwelled on earth. His responsibilities included establishing the lifestyle of Heaven on earth by ensuring the divine constitution of existence is adhered to in accordance with the divine mind. That was an enviable position of unrivalled splendour!

> *"I appointed a winged creature to guard your home on my holy mountain, where you walked among gems that dazzled like fire"* *(Eze.28:14 CEV).*

'A winged creature' refers to a cherub. Ezekiel chapter 28 verse 14 reveals that Lucifer had cherubs that waited on him. That is, other Morning Stars were under his authority.

Interestingly, not only was Lucifer a chief cherub, he was also an anointed one. The term 'anointed' in Ezekiel chapter 28 verse 14 is from the Hebrew word *mimshach*, which literally means 'expansion or expanded influence.' Lucifer had an expanded authority over many other angels. That is, he was an archangel with expanded influence over many other subordinate angels.

Furthermore, 'anointing' refers to the power of the Spirit of God. Lucifer was anointed by God to preside over a realm of creation on behalf of God. His delegated authority from God was apparently on earth, where he exercised himself as the Prince on behalf of God. Since he was a Cherub and an Archangel, Lucifer had the authority to enforce the Law of God among the then dwellers on earth. By so doing, he would ensure that the glory of God fill the earth. He was the Shining One whose duty was to bear and enforce the light of Jehovah the Creator around the earth.

Indeed, Lucifer was entrusted with the divine mandate of defending and expanding the worship of God on earth. Being the anointed covering cherub, Lucifer was the Custodian of the Divine Constitution on the then earth. The Revised Standard Version (RSV) translated it as 'anointed guardian cherub' (Eze.28:14). Lucifer guarded and enforced God's Law among the nations of the sons of God on the then earth and at the same time had access to the Throne of God in Heaven.

In other words, he was the Prime Minister of God entrusted with the sensitive role of the defence of the Divine Constitution on the then earth. As the defender or protector of the Divine Constitution, he had direct access to the Throne of God in Heaven. He could easily move from the then earth to Heaven and present at the Throne of God to behold the very face of the Ancient of Days, a privilege not enjoyed by many angels. Indeed, Lucifer had access to the holy mountain of God and walked in the midst of fiery stones, referring to the Throne of the Most High God with its fiery presence.

> *"You were the anointed cherub who covers;*
> *I established you;*
> *You were on the holy mountain of God;*
> *You walked back and forth in the midst of fiery stones"*
> *(Eze.28: 14 NKJV).*

Lucifer was made by God to be the Governor of the World, the Prince of the Earth. With his great wisdom and dexterity, he commanded attention on Earth and in Heaven. Indeed, he had influence and authority on Earth and in Heaven, which is the headquarters of the universe.

The Origin of Sin

CHAPTER 8
THE SEED OF EVIL

SADLY, LUCIFER'S AUTHORITY, BEAUTY, AND intelligence caused him to start thinking of himself more highly than he should have. He started nursing the idea of someday being the lord of all, even lording over his Creator. He wanted to be the standard of measurement and centre of reference instead of his Creator God. In other words, Lucifer allowed the seed of pride to be born and gradually infiltrate his heart. He had allowed his authority, beauty, and intelligence to breed pride in him.

> *"You were blameless in your ways from the day you were created until iniquity and guilt were found in you" (Eze.28:15 AMP)*

HOW SEED OF INIQUITY ENTERED LUCIFER'S HEART

Many usually ask who planted iniquity in Lucifer's heart if he was created a perfect being. Where did the pride come from to enter into his perfectly created nature?

The answer is that all sons of God, angels or humans, were created as moral beings with the capability of making choices and decisions. At the Beginning Era, there was no evil whatsoever in God's creation. All were pure and in harmony with God's laws of perfection. However, Lucifer, seeing the beauty of the glory of divinity and the omnipotent power that God commanded across the expanse of His creation, became jealous. He felt that with his authority, beauty, and intelligence he could persuade, cajole, and even force other Morning Stars to follow him as their ultimate leader and abandon the Creator God.

As a moral being, Lucifer had the power of choice. He was never created as a puppet to follow divine order sheepishly. No, not at all! Like every other son of God, Lucifer was a moral being with a heart and an active mind. His mind could choose to follow the divine order or rebel against it. Sadly, he rather chose to allow the desire to command the sole attention and obeisance of all and sundry, including his Creator, to start welling up in his heart. It was a desire of a selfish ambition. That was the seed of pride, a contaminant that would soon permeate God's perfect realms of creation, and things would never be the same again!

Because such a thought was abnormal to the perfect laws that have been governing God's creation, it was inappropriate, and it was called 'evil.' Thus, a new term, 'evil,' entered into the vocabulary of creation. An 'evil' means something contrary and malevolent to the established order.

"You were blameless in your ways from the day you were created until iniquity and guilt were found in you" (Eze.28:15 AMP).

Note the word 'iniquity' in the above Scripture; it is etymologically from two words 'en,' which means opposite or contrary, and 'equity,' which means fairness or justice. Thus, 'iniquity' simply means 'contrary to fairness' or 'opposition to justice.' Iniquity is evil, meaning it is something contrary and malevolent to the established order. Lucifer had allowed his heart to entertain a thought that deviated from the perfect harmony of creation, hence, it was an evil thought. It was a thought of iniquity, which is evil. The opposite of evil is good. That is how the seed of evil was born in Lucifer's heart.

The Lure of Power

In other words, Lucifer started secretly nursing seed of rebellion against the supreme authority of God. As a moral being, Lucifer had the innate ability, the willpower, to reject such an evil thought in his heart. Instead, the thought passed down from his heart to his mind, and he allowed his mind to process this seed of evil.

As a moral agent with a free will, he could have nipped this evil in the bud so that his mind wouldn't process it any further. He could have stopped his mind and heart from drifting aside from God's Law. But he did not. Thus, Lucifer's mind started brooding on this abnormal seed in his heart. The lure of power with total plenipotentiary and supremacy did not allow him to extinguish the propagation of this evil seed. The seed of evil was, therefore, born in God's perfect creation.

The book of Ezekiel chapter 14 succinctly captured this:

> *"Your heart was proud and arrogant because of your beauty; you destroyed your wisdom for the sake of your splendour"*
>
> *(Eze.28:17a AMP).*

> *"It was your good looks that made you arrogant, and you were so famous that you started acting like a fool" (Eze.28:17a CEV).*

LUCIFER'S EVIL PLOT

Lucifer did not only conceive an evil thought in his heart, but his mind also started strategizing how to actualise this evil desire. According to the Scriptures, Lucifer's plotted to take over three strategic positions:

(a) Highest Throne

Lucifer's first plot was to take over the Throne of God, the headquarters of the universe. He wanted to exalt himself above all the Morning Stars including all his peers, the archangels. He was not satisfied with the level of the delegated authority he commanded; he wanted all of the grandeur and pomp of the offices of the other archangels. He wasn't satisfied with being an Anointed Covering

Cherub, but he wanted the complete and full allegiance of all. Simply put, Lucifer wanted totalitarian power; he wanted power that would give him total control of the entire realm of creation including power over his Creator!

By his great wisdom, Lucifer knew that a successful life was not about occupation of office and holding titles, but rather to successfully perform the assigned duty of the office and be a blessing to the people he was assigned to. However, he corrupted his wisdom by allowing the seed of evil to grow in him, thereby choosing to ignore the truth.

> *"You, the bright morning star, ...you said to yourself, 'I'll climb to heaven*
> *and place my throne above the highest stars'" (Isa.14:12,13 CEV).*

> *"O Lucifer, son of the morning! you have said in your heart: 'I will ascend into heaven, I will exalt my throne above the stars of God'" (Isa.14:12,13 NKJV).*

As discussed in Chapter 3, 'stars' here refer to the sons of God that carry the very life of God (*zoe*) in them. That is, Lucifer's first plot was to exalt himself above all the sons of God and then set up his throne in Heaven, thereby displacing God's Throne. In other words, he wanted the power that God exercised. Lucifer was not contented with the delegated power given to him; he wanted all of the authority and to be placed above everyone else. What selfishness!

(b) Lord of Worship

Lucifer plotted to receive worship from every other Morning Star and the Creator Himself. He wanted such solemnity and total commitment from everyone including God. His proud heart made him to neglect the fact that he was a creature with limitedness unlike the infinite Creator that deserves all the worship. He wanted everyone including God to bow down and worship him! He wanted to be the Lord of the universe, commanding the attention of all including God.

> *"You, the bright morning star,...you said to yourself, 'I'll sit there with the gods far away in the north'" (Isa.14:12,13 CEV)*

The 'north' in Scriptures often refers to the place where Heaven and the Throne of God are situated (Psa.48:1,2). The 'gods' here actually means 'congregation' or 'assembly' as translated in many other Bible versions such as NKJV. Often congregation refers to assembly of worship. In other words, Lucifer was coveting the worship that was meant for God alone.

> *"O Lucifer, son of the morning!... For you have said in your heart: 'I will also sit on the mount of the congregation, on the farthest sides of the north'" (Isa.14:12,13 NKJV)*

(c) The New 'God' of Creation

The ultimate plan of Lucifer was to enthrone himself as the new god of the creation. Lucifer was not omnipotent, omniscient, or omnipresent; he had limited authority. The authority he had was the one delegated to him by his Creator. Lucifer was not all-wise and was not all-seeing like God. It might have baffled the imagination of most sons of God then that Lucifer would ever dare to dream and entertain such thoughts of dethroning God.

> *"O Lucifer, son of the morning!... For you have said in your heart: 'I will be like the Most High'" (Isa.14:12,13 NKJV)*

Thus, the eventual plan of Lucifer was to exalt himself above the clouds, referring to the glory of God. He wanted glory, which means the magnificence and splendour of God.

> *"O Lucifer, son of the morning!... For you have said in your heart:*
> *'I will also sit on the mount of the congregation, on the farthest*
> *sides of the north; I will ascend above the heights of the clouds'"*
>
> *(Isa.14:12,13 NKJV).*

In summary, Lucifer wanted the Power, Worship, and Glory of God, which are the very essence of God; the attributes that make God the Most High. That is, Lucifer wanted to be 'god the most high.' All his words were in the first person pronoun 'I'. He wanted all for himself and himself alone, a contrastingly opposite character of God. His selfishly megalomaniacal desire was to dethrone God and become the Most High. Simply put, Lucifer wanted to be the new 'God.'

CHAPTER 9

THE FIRST TREASON IN CREATION

How long Lucifer nursed and incubated this evil plot in his heart we do not know. But certainly the Most High God who created the heart knew the secrets of Lucifer's heart. By His patience, God allowed Lucifer to rethink and repent of his evil desire, and to seek for forgiveness. Instead, Lucifer went ahead with his evil intention. In His omniscience, God allowed Lucifer's evil devices to become full-blown.

Lucifer soon started to execute his hideous plot, gradually infiltrating the minds of some of his fellow Morning Stars with his evil plot. Slowly, he started winning some of them to his side. How long this plot lasted was unknown to this side of eternity, but it appears to be quite lengthy, possibly hundreds of years.

Not long thereafter, about 33 percent population of Morning Stars was won over by Lucifer in preparation for their final onslaught (Rev.12:4). Thirty-three percent was a huge number considering the large population of angels, which according to Scriptures seems to be in billions (Rev.5: 11).

THE IMPACT ON THE EARTH

Lucifer's treacherous activities caused disunity and discord among the Morning Stars that dwelt on earth and the angelic population in general. The two-third of Morning Stars and the other angelic beings who refused to bow to the pressure of Lucifer found themselves in opposition and antagonism to Lucifer's loyalists. Acrimony set in and the earth was no longer the one beautiful, harmonious place to dwell in. Lucifer had done injustice to God's perfect creation.

"O Lucifer, son of the morning!... You who weakened the nations!"
(Isa.14:12 NKJV).

Lucifer supplanted divine laws and corrupted the abiding constitutions that governed existence on earth. With such appalling acts, he went about desecrating the very tenets he was created to uphold and protect. Because he was the Anointed Guardian Cherub, the Protector of the Divine Constitution, he attempted to twist the laws for his own personal benefits, thereby, engineering corruption on earth.

"By the multitude of your iniquities, in the unrighteousness of your trade you profaned your sanctuaries...All who know you among the peoples are appalled at you..." (Eze.28:18,19 RSV).

THE FIRST WAR IN CREATION

Finally, with his 33 percent dissident loyal converts, Lucifer launched a revolt against God. With such audacity, Lucifer took the revolt to the Seat of Divinity, Heaven. What an arrogant effrontery! A creature challenging his Creator! God did not need to fight back, only a word from the Most High could eliminate the very existence of these rebels. However, for a fair contest, God allowed some of the remaining two-third (about 67 percent) loyal Morning Stars and other angelic beings, headed by the archangel Michael, to quell the uprising.

"And there was war in heaven: Michael and his angels fought against the dragon; and the dragon fought and his angels, and prevailed not; neither was their place found any more in heaven. And the great dragon was cast out, that old serpent, called the Devil, and Satan, which deceiveth the whole world: he was cast out into the earth, and his angels were cast out with him" (Rev.12:7-9 KJV).

Note Apostle John wrote about this event in the Bible book of Revelation centuries after it had occurred. God revealed to John what happened during that period while the Beloved Apostle was in exile at the Patmos Island in about AD 100 because of anti-Christian persecution under the Roman emperor Domitian (see SSB Book 6).

The Outcome of the First War

Michael and his loyal team won the battle against Lucifer and his angels, and this was vividly rendered in CEV translation:

"A war broke out in heaven. Michael and his angels were fighting against the dragon and its angels. But the dragon lost the battle. It and its angels were forced out of their places in heaven and were thrown down to the earth. Yes, that old snake and his angels were thrown out of heaven! That snake, who fools everyone on earth, is known as the devil and Satan" (Rev.12:7-9 CEV).

Fig.8: Lucifer deceived about 33 percent of his colleagues, the Morning Stars, to launch an insurrection against God; hence, divine judgment awaited the rebels!

CHAPTER 10

THE DIVINE JUDGMENT OF LUCIFER

GOD IS A GOD OF justice, and justice demands that every disobedience must suffer its consequences. Lucifer hatched a wicked plot, drew about 33 percent of his colleagues into the schism, but failed to win the resultant battle. Hence, the righteous laws of creation must take their course; Lucifer must bear the consequences of his rebellion. Thus, divine judgment was handed down on him, and this can be grouped into three categories as follows:

(1) DETHRONEMENT

Lucifer was dethroned from his enviable position as the Anointed Covering Cherub. He ceased to be the Chief Cherub in charge of protecting and guarding divine sacredness. From thence, he was no longer the Custodian of God's Law, the Divine Constitution.

> *"How you are fallen from heaven,*
> *O Lucifer, son of the morning!*
> *How you are cut down to the ground,*
> *You who weakened the nations!" (Isa.14:12 NKJV)*

Hence, for eternity, Lucifer's position as the Anointed Covering Cherub ceased. Never again will he be the Prime Minister of Divinity, and he ceased to be the Chief Morning Star; rather he would now be the Wandering Star (Jud.1:13).

Prophet Ezekiel was given a glimpse of the outcome of this judgment:

"Through your widespread trade you were filled with violence, and you sinned. So I drove you in disgrace from the mount of God, and I expelled you, guardian cherub, from among the fiery stones. Your heart became proud on account of your beauty, and you corrupted your wisdom because of your splendour. So I threw you to the earth; I made a spectacle of you before kings"

(Ezek.28:16 NIV).

According to Ezekiel chapter 28 verse 16, Lucifer were defeated and thrown out of the Mount of God (referring to the Throne of God in Heaven). The once powerful and influential prince, the Covering Cherub, was disgraced and made a spectacle of ridicule among the 'kings' of the earth. The kings of the earth refer to the highly placed Morning Stars that ruled the various nations on earth with Lucifer as their Prime Minister.

(2) LOSS OF DIVINE SONSHIP

Not only did Lucifer lose his position of influence, but he also lost his sonship status. The life of God (*zoe*) stopped flowing through him.

"By the multitude of your iniquities, in the unrighteousness of your trade you profaned your sanctuaries; so I brought forth fire from the midst of you; it consumed you, and I turned you to ashes upon the earth in the sight of all who saw you" (Eze.28:18 RSV).

To destroy the *zoe* flowing through his body, God sent a divine fire to devour Lucifer. The judgmental fire of God destroyed and consumed Lucifer's nature completely, as clearly stated in Ezekiel chapter 28 verse 18. It was a divine judgment with total destruction.

A permanent genetic alteration of his nature occurred. No more would Lucifer ever be the son of God with *zoe* flowing through him again. Rather in his new nature flows a life that stands in complete contrast to the once *zoe* life in him. He had ceased to be Lucifer, the Shining One, forever! This new nature is a complete opposite of the *zoe* nature. It is what is now called 'sin.' Sin is the opposite of *zoe*.

(3) DEATH

"The wages of sin is death" (Rom.6:23). This is a divine law. It is called the Law of Sin and Death (Rom.8:2). According to this divine law, wherever there is sin, death is the ultimate consequence.

Lucifer had allowed a deviated pattern of thought to build up in him, culminating in treasonable acts that were contrary to divine order. Consequently, divine judgment of fire had incinerated him, completely transforming his nature and permanently disfiguring his life, which now stood in complete opposition to divine life. By the divine law, this opposite nature, known as sin, ultimately attracts death. Thus, Lucifer must die, and die he did.

Thus, one of the divine judgments against Lucifer was death. He died both physically and spiritually.

> *"All who know you among the peoples are appalled at you; you have come to a dreadful end and shall be no more for ever"*
> *(Eze.28:19 RSV).*

Physical Death of Lucifer
The physical death of Lucifer was that his beautifully exquisite body died and decayed into ashes to become part of the earth's material, where it was once formed from. Lucifer's body, thus, became dust of the earth.

"By the multitude of your iniquities, in the unrighteousness of your trade you profaned your sanctuaries; so I brought forth fire from the midst of you; it consumed you, and I turned you to ashes upon the earth in the sight of all who saw you" (Eze.28:18 RSV).

The physical body is a covering for the spirit. Physical death means that the physical body dies and is separated from its spirit. A spirits does not die physically. Lucifer's body died, and its spirit lives on. That is, Lucifer spirit now lives without its beautiful body. Lucifer's spirit is what we now called **Satan**, which has the nature known as **sin**. In other words, the life that flows in Satan is called sin. Satan is from the Hebrew word 'satan,' which means 'an adversary, one who withstands.' In the New Testament, Satan is from the Aramaic word 'satanas,' which also means 'an adversary.'

Satan is an adversary of divinity, an adversary of good things, an adversary of righteousness. Sin, Satan's life, is the opposite of zoe, the life of God; hence, the nature of sin is an adversary to the divine laws of creation.

Spiritual Death of Lucifer

Spiritual death means to be totally cut off from the Source of life, God. That is, when spiritual death occurs, the being has no more contact with God, the Source of life. The opposite of life is death. Lucifer did not only physically, but he also died spiritually. His spirit, called Satan, has been cut off from the Source of life.

In Satan there was no any atom or trace of divine life. He had been spiritually cut off from God. Once a son of God with zoe life, now Satan has an adversary nature, sin. Satan is also called the Devil, the accuser or slanderer. This was why when Satan appeared in Heaven among other angels at the time of Job to accuse or slander Job's reputation, Satan was not addressed as a 'son of God' like the other angels.

"Now there was a day when the sons of God came to present themselves before the Lord, and Satan also came among them"
(Job 1: 6 RSV).

Satan is not and can never be a son of God. He does not have any form of divine nature again. For instance, Satan does not know what is called mercy, love, justice, peace, et cetera, which are all attributes of divinity. Rather Satan's nature is stark evil. As stated on Page 68, an 'evil' means something contrary and malevolent to the established order of divinity. Satan's nature is a stark opposite of divinity. The opposite of evil is good. Satan does not have any iota of goodness in him.

This is why humans who have come in contact with Satan are often appalled at the level of evil expressed by Satan. He, Satan, enjoys when there is suffering, and does not have any trace of compassion or love towards another being. His language is lies as he speaks lies effortlessly. He ravishes in violence and destruction as murder is part of his evil nature.

THE ORIGIN OF HELL

According to the Law of Life, all spirit beings possess life and, hence, live eternally. In other words, God created each spirit being to be like Him in existence. God is a Spirit and lives forever, hence, once created, a spirit lives forever. Satan is the defamed spirit of Lucifer and has the ability to live forever. However, since he was no longer having zoe, the divine life, flowing in him, he must be cast to a region where there was no iota of divine life.

In other words, Satan could no longer live on earth or in Heaven, which are abodes teeming with the life of God. Thus, a new abode that has no form of divine life whatsoever and not a single iota of divine presence would need to be prepared for him. This new lifeless abode is what is called **Hell**.

"Yet thou shalt be brought down to Hell, to the sides of the pit"
(Isa.14:15 KJV).

Hell was prepared by God primarily for Satan and the rebellious angels. Jesus clearly stated this in one of His teachings:

"Then He will also say to those on the left hand, 'Depart from Me, you cursed, into the everlasting fire [Hell] prepared for the devil and his angels'" (Mat.25:41 NKJV).

Thus, Satan's new abode now is Hell. He lives in Hell now and no longer on earth or in Heaven. Hell is a a gigantic pit of fire that burns with sulphur and brimstone with no iota of divine life, but rather dryness, emptiness, lonesomeness, blackness and sorrow with worms that never die.

From this new abode of Hell, Satan accesses both earth, Heaven, and other realms of God's creation. For instance, as discussed in Chapter 19, he was in the Garden of Eden on Earth as the Serpent (Gen. chpt. 3), years after he was cast into his new home, Hell. Today he occasionally travels out of his home, Hell, to roam to and fro on the earth.

Also, God still allows him to ascend to Heaven from time to time, where he goes to slander and accuse sons of God.

"Now there was a day when the sons of God came to present themselves before the Lord, and Satan also came among them. And the Lord said to Satan, 'From where do you come?' So Satan answered the Lord and said, 'From going to and fro on the earth, and from walking back and forth on it'" (Job 1:6,7 NKJV).

Fig.9: Satan the Devil
The judgmental fire of God destroyed and consumed Lucifer's nature completely. A permanent genetic alteration of his nature occurred. Forever, he had ceased to be Lucifer, the Shining One!

Lucifer's body died, and its spirit lives on, and that is what is now called Satan, which has the nature known as sin. Satan is not and can never be a son of God. He does not have any form of divine nature again. Rather Satan's nature is stark evil, the very opposite of good.

THE LAKE OF FIRE: A LAND-OF-NO-RETURN

Why does God allow Satan to roam out of his abode, Hell? Why didn't God confine Satan permanently in Hell? The answer is that so that throughout eternity, creation will see what rebellion and its consequences can cause. Satan is a stark reminder of the consequences of following the path of rebellion against divine order. However, one day, Satan and all his followers that bear his sin-genome will be cast into the **Lake of Fire**, a part of Hell where condemned beings are cast into for eternal forgetfulness and everlasting destruction. Apostle John had a vision of this in about AD 100:

> "And the devil who had deceived them was hurled into the lake of fire and burning brimstone (sulfur), where the beast (Antichrist) and false prophet are also; and they will be tormented day and night, forever and ever. Then death and Hades [the realm of the dead] were thrown into the lake of fire. This is the second death, the lake of fire [the eternal separation from God]
>
> (Rev.20:10,14 AMP).

This means that the part of Hell Satan is kept presently still offers him the opportunity of travelling in and out to other worlds such as the Earth and Heaven. But once in the Lake of Fire, there will not be any opportunity of travelling. The Lake of Fire is a Land-of-No-Return.

About 33 percent of the Morning Stars joined Lucifer in his evil plot, as discussed in Chapter 9. These dissident sons of God also received the appropriate divine judgment. Their judgment was akin to that of their leader, Lucifer.

(1) LOSS OF DIVINE SONSHIP

These Morning Stars were sons of God with *zoe*, the life of God, flowing through each of them. However, following their rebellious action with Lucifer, and eventual defeat, they lost their sonship. Just like Lucifer, the fire of God fell, destroyed and consumed them completely. It was a divine judgment with utter destruction. No more would they ever be the sons of God with zoe flowing through them.

Like Lucifer, their leader, the nature of these Morning Stars underwent permanent genetic alteration resulting in complete contrast to the previous *zoe* life in them. Zoe life stopped flowing through them. In place of *zoe* was the new nature of sin, much the same as in their fallen hero, Lucifer.

(2) BANISHMENT FROM HEAVEN

These dissident Morning Stars were banished from having access to the Throne of God. No longer would they be citizens of Heaven and members of the Commonwealth of God. They ceased from being part of God; they could not appear in Heaven any more. It was a total banishment from Heaven all through the remaining eternal period of their existence.

(3) DEATH

Like Lucifer, the ultimate recompense of sinful acts of these fallen morning stars was death because *"the wages of sin is death"* (Rom.6:23 KJV). That is, the Law of Sin and Death must take its due course. These dissident Morning Stars had to die just as Lucifer. And they died both physically and spiritually.

The Physical Death of the Dissident Morning Stars

The physical death of these dissident Morning Stars was the death of their bodies or physical existence. Like Lucifer, they died physically and their bodies decayed in the earth. But their spirits live on. These spirits are now called **Demons**. Thus, demons are the spirits of the fallen angels that rebelled with Lucifer.

The term demon is from the Greek word *daimonion*, which appears 63 times in the New Testament, and it means 'evil spirits or the messengers and ministers of the devil.' In the Old Testament, they are simply referred to as **evil spirits**. That is, their nature is now ultra-evil just as their master, Satan, and stands in complete contrast to the nature of God.

Categories of Demons

Though the Scriptures did not mention the names of these fallen Morning Stars, who are now called demons, yet the Scriptures describe them by their functions, which include the followings:

• Deceiving Spirits

Deceiving spirits are demons that specialise in misrepresentation of truths (1Kin.22:21-23). Divination, occultism, fortune-telling, astrology, sorcery, and magic, use deceiving spirits a lot to attempt to predict the future. God forbids all these practices because they are demonic in origin (Deut.18:10-12).

Deceiving spirits are demons that cause confusion and disorderliness in the minds of people resulting in strife and contention. They cause confusion in peoples' minds so that they do not heed the Gospel warning and the way of God, but rather choose to follow the devil (Isa.19:14; Rom.1:17-32). Deceiving spirits are also called the *Spirits of Error* because they seek to twist the truth ultimately produce errors (1Joh.4:6). For example, Elymas the Sorcerer used a deceiving spirit to lead indigenes of the Greek island of Paphos to advance his trade (Act.13: 4-12).

Deceiving spirits breed false doctrines and they are deceiving the world into adopting false religions instead of following the true God, thereby rejecting the salvation plan of God for mankind through the Saviour Jesus Christ. A good example was the slave girl with a divination spirit that successfully deceived the people of Philippi, a city in Macedonia, to believe in false worship of the true God. It was the arrival of Apostle Paul and Silas in the city with the Gospel in AD 49 that exposed such deceit, and the Apostle finally cast out the deceiving spirit from the girl (Act.16:16-19). Because they are behind the formation of ideologies and religious fanaticism, deceiving spirits are also called *Religious Spirits.*

• Familiar Spirits

Familiar spirits are demons that mimic the lifestyle or physique of a person or object. Necromancy, which is conjuration of the spirits of the dead for purposes of magically revealing the future or influencing the course of events, and other forms of Spiritism are often practiced with familiar spirits. For example, the Witch of Endor used familiar spirit (1Sam. chpt. 28).

Ancestral worship is a widespread practise in Africa and in many other parts of the world. A cardinal feature of such practice is the conjuration of the spirits of the dead. This conjuration is done with the help of familiar demonic spirits. Hence, ancestral worship is inimical to the true worship of Jehovah God, the Maker of Heaven and earth. Wise people will stay away from all such practices, which may appear harmless at the surface but heavily rooted in demonism that ultimately brings heartaches, failure, peril, and destruction.

• Mammon Spirits

Mammon spirits are demons that produce the love of money in the hearts of people. The Scriptures categorically states that "the love of money is the root of all evils" (1Tim.6:10). Unknown to some people, the Bible does not say that money is the root of all evils, rather it is 'the love of money' that is the root of all evils.

Mammon spirits capture the hearts and minds of men to love money instead of loving God. These spirits cause men to value money above God and human life, causing the individuals to disregard established safe orders while in desperate hot pursuit of money. To love money is to worship money rather than God (Mat.6:24).

• Spirits of Bondage

These are demonic spirits that produce addictions of all kinds such as addiction to immoral life (Rom.8:15). Some cases of drug addiction, alcoholism, illicit sexual cravings, binge consumption, et cetera, are rooted in demonic attacks, which may be oppression, obsession, or outright possession of the human being. Spirit of Bondage is also known as *Spirit of Addiction*.

Spirits of bondage produce negative habits that victims are unable to come out of them. In such situations, no amount of psychotherapy or medical intervention can produce a permanent solution; only the liberating power of Christ can break such negative habits and set the victims free.

• Spirits of Infirmity

Spirits of infirmity are demons that produce all manners of diseases in the body and mind of people. An eighteen-year inability to walk straight, which we will today possibly diagnosed as arthritis, in an Israelite woman was caused by a spirit of infirmity, which Jesus drove out of the woman in AD 32 (Luk.13:10-17).

• Whoredom Spirits

Whoredom spirits are demons that cause sexual perversion. Fornication, adultery, homosexuality, and bestiality are often produced by the whoredom spirits (Hos.4:12; 5:4). They are also called *Unclean Spirits* because they can produce all manners of unclean habits and lifestyles (Mar.6:7; Luk.11:24-26).

THREE FORMS OF DEMONIC ATTACK

Note that demons are real and they do attack humans. Many cases of misfortunes, disasters, addictions, diseases, et cetera, are direct impact or attacks of demonic presence. Demonic attacks can be any of these three forms:

Obsession: this is when a demon infiltrates the thought life of the individual so that the victim feels incapacitated in controlling his thought on a particular issue. Such thoughts include suicidal ideation, immoral cravings, abnormal thought of illness, et cetera.

Oppression: this is when a demon attacks an individual directly and leaves the individual once the demon has achieved its goal(s), which may be to cause bodily ailment, addiction to substances, et cetera. This can happen repeatedly with the ultimate goal being to possess the individual.

Possession: this is when a demon enters and resides inside the body of the individual.

Demons, like their leader Satan, are thieves; the ultimate goal of a demonic attack is to destroy its victim, for *"the thief does not come except to steal, and to kill, and to destroy"* (Joh.10:10 NKJV). A demonic attack, whether obsession, oppression, or outright possession, do not have medical solution. Psychotherapy, sedation, electroconvulsive therapy, and any other medical therapy do not have lasting effect on demonic attack. Only the anointing of the Holy Spirit in the Name of Jesus Christ can set the victim free as evidenced by the following story of Johan.

Johan's Story of Demonic Presence

Johan was a university student. On campus, he got involved with some bad gangs and was caught up in drugs. Soon the drugs affected him as he spent his school fees on his addiction and wayward living. He could not afford to keep his sexual life under check as he jumped from one woman to another so that he was openly known to be a serial womaniser. This habit was complicated by the fact that he was also caught up in alcoholism. Due to his wayward lifestyle, he abandoned his varsity education in his third year, just a year to his graduation.

According to Johan, he had tried several times to rid himself of his addiction and sexual perversion. In addition, his family had taken him for medical assistance. He visited psychologists a number of times, but that could not help him. His case appeared hopeless medically.

I met him in our clinic in 2001. He had contracted a sexually transmitted disease, had infected wounds all around his legs, and looked quite unkempt and carefree. At the clinic, I tried to be a bit friendly and Johan opened up telling me his story. As at then, he had no vision and no plan for his life. I invited him to Church. He came under the conviction of the Holy Spirit during the Church Sunday worship, and he decided to surrender his life to Jesus. When he did this, a remarkable thing happened to him!

His abnormal cravings for sexual gratification and his desire for alcoholism and drugs just died off. Initially, he thought that might be a temporal relief. But weeks rolled by, and still the abnormal habits were dead in him. When I saw him about three months later, he told me that the smell of liquor even made him to feel nauseous. What a transformation! Praise be to God!

Johan later met and joined a professional and businessmen Christian fellowship, which kindled his interest to surrender his future totally to Jesus and quit his wayward lifestyle. Subsequently, he went back and finished his education, even did his Master's degree, married with a lovely family, and started a business.

His story is a testimony of the power of Christ in breaking addictions. Johan's involvement with some bad gangs on campus opened him up to demonic attack. However, the power of Christ destroyed the demonic stronghold on Johan and set him free, and this can happen to any victim of addiction, or any case of demonic attack, if he or she will invite Jesus into his or her life. Remember, Christ is not a thief like Satan and demons; He will only come in when invited (Mat.11:28-30).

THE SPIRITUAL DEATH OF THE DISSIDENT MORNING STARS

Another divine judgment of these dissident Morning Stars, who have become demons, was that they died spiritually. Spiritual death is total separation from divine life. Thus, as with Satan, Hell was prepared by God for these demons. Hell is now their home. It is a place devoid of any form of divine life. It is a dreadful place, far more dreadful than any human imagination. Hence, these fallen angels were banished to Hell. Apostle Peter vividly captured this in his epistle:

> "God did not spare even the angels who sinned. He threw them into hell, in gloomy pits of darkness, where they are being held until the Day of Judgment" (2Pet.2:4 NLT).

The 'Day of Judgment' mentioned in the above Scripture (2Pet.2:4 NLT) refers to the day when these demons with their leader, Satan, will finally be destroyed and be cast into the Lake of Fire (Rev.20:10,14). The Lake of Fire is for the condemned. The sentence of condemnation is for any being that carries the sin-genome in his nature because Hell is the home prepared for sin-laden beings. The Hell's Lake of Fire is a place of eternal hopelessness, endless suffering, and everlasting forgetfulness. Hell is real; it is as real as our physical planet Earth. As mentioned above, Hell was not originally prepared for humans but for the dissident Lucifer and the rebellious Morning Stars. The existence of Hell is a warning and a chilling realisation that should drive any person not to follow the part of these fallen angels.

Chapter 12

The World of the Fallen Lucifer

The nefarious activities of Lucifer and his dissident Morning Stars impacted negatively on the earth. Cruelty and evil infiltrated the once harmonious earth. Corruption, violence, factions, and many other vices that were not before in God's perfect creation now perverted the surface of the earth. Commercial activities were filled with venalities and profanity. The worship of God was corrupted as Lucifer sought to force the loyal Morning Stars to join his evil course.

> *"By the multitude of your iniquities, in the unrighteousness of your trade you profaned your sanctuaries..." (Eze.28:18 RSV).*

The insurrection activities of Lucifer and his dissident Morning Stars left the then Earth defaced and vandalised. The earth became filled with the atrocities of Lucifer and his fallen angels. Thus, the purpose of the creation of the earth had been abused. Lucifer had succeeded in infiltrating the whole earth with his evil life of sin. The various nations on the then earth were filled with the cruelty and evils of these seditious Morning Stars.

In summary, the whole earth was infiltrated with odours of sacrilege, corruption and profanity. Therefore, the earth had to be destroyed in order to wipe off the evil from its surface.

DIVINE JUDGMENT OF THE FIRST EARTH

The Scriptures give us insight into the divine judgment that was meted out to the then Earth. God destroyed the Earth and covered it with water.

Genesis chapter one verse one refers to the Beginning Era when God created the Earth and Heaven and filled them with sons of God, the Morning Stars.

> *"In the beginning God created the heavens and the earth" (Gen.1:1 NIV).*

Interestingly, verse two of the same Genesis chapter one mentions that the beautifully created Earth was now formless and empty.

> *"Now the earth was formless and empty, darkness was over the surface of the deep, and the Spirit of God was hovering over the waters" (Gen.1:2 NIV).*

That has raised the curiosity of many scholars for centuries. The common question has been: How could God create the heavens and the earth and left them formless and void? To leave the created heavens and earth formless and void with water and thick darkness being the only inhabitants could not be in keeping with the character of Jehovah Elohim, the God of purpose and beauty.

However, what we must know is that the time frame between verses one and two of Genesis chapter one refers to the Luciferic period when the Morning Stars were created and filled the earth. Thus, between verse one and verse two of Genesis chapter one was the interlude era during which the created Earth was filled with Lucifer and his fellow sons of God, some who revolted against God – the revolt being led by Lucifer. In a bid to enforce and achieve their selfish ambitions, Lucifer and his group resorted to threats, corrupt practices, and sacrilege, against the divine order of perfection, thereby infiltrating the earth with all manners of vices. As a consequence of all these atrocities, divine judgment came upon them and the beautiful earth was destroyed by God and covered with water. Thus, Genesis chapter one verse two refers to the destruction of the created Earth.

"Now the earth was formless and empty, darkness was over the surface of the deep, and the Spirit of God was hovering over the waters" (Gen.1:2 NIV).

A Glimpse of the Destruction

Following the destruction, the earth became formless and void. However, there is no Scripture that mentions that the Third Heaven, the Seat of the Universe, was destroyed along with the earth. Apparently, Lucifer's insurrection did not affect Heaven, where the Throne of God is situated. Only the Earth and possibly the first and second heavens (referring to the galaxies) perished and were covered with water.

Prophet Jeremiah was given a glimpse of this destruction by God. He wrote in about 620 BC:

"I looked at the earth, and it was formless and empty; and at the heavens, and their light was gone. I looked at the mountains, and they were quaking; all the hills were swaying. I looked, and there were no people; every bird in the sky had flown away. I looked, and the fruitful land was a desert all its towns lay in ruins before the Lord, before his fierce anger" (Jer.4:23-26 NIV).

Note that this Scripture in Jeremiah chapter 4 was not referring to a coming event. It is in past tense, referring to something that had happened. Prophet Jeremiah declared that the earth was destroyed and there were no people; their towns and fruitful land completely laid in waste. The heavenly lights (referring to the stars and moons) and the birds were all perished by the fierce anger of the Lord.

Obviously, these were not referring to Noah's Flood in which the birds and eight people (Noah's household) were saved and not destroyed. However, in this case reported by Prophet Jeremiah, no people and birds were saved. The only event of this proportion and magnitude was the destruction of the earth of the Luciferic era. God was taking Prophet Jeremiah back to events of thousands (possibly millions) of years before the arrival of man, much like what God did to Moses on Mount Sinai when He took Moses back almost 2000 years of human history into the Garden of Eden to view Adam and Eve, the first human family, in which Moses documented in the Book of Genesis. Only God can do such things because He was there in all of these events. That is His omniscience in action!

By showing Prophet Jeremiah the events of several years of the pre-human Luciferic era, God was also letting the Prophet to know what will happen to our present earth as a warning to Israel and the rest of humanity. Indeed, the subsequent verses after verse 26 of Jeremiah chapter 4 confirm this:

"This is what the Lord says: The whole land will be ruined, though I will not destroy it completely. Therefore, the earth will mourn and the heavens above grow dark, because I have spoken and will not relent, I have decided and will not turn back" (Jer.4:27,28 NIV).

Thus, Jeremiah chapter 4 verses 1 to 22 refer to the sinful acts of man, verses 23 to 26 reminding humans of what happened to the Lucifer's era, while verses 27 and 28 warning humans that such fate will befall humanity due to the perpetuation of sin on earth.

Fig.10: In about 620 BC, God opened the eyes of young Prophet Jeremiah to see the events of several thousands of years of the pre-human Luciferic era during which God destroyed the first earth and covered it with water as a result of the rebellion of Lucifer. By showing Prophet Jeremiah the events of the pre-human Luciferic era, God was also letting the Prophet to know what will happen to our present earth as a warning to us all of the consequence of rebellion against the Creator.

WHERE ARE THE LOYAL MORNING STARS?

What happened to the two-third Morning Stars who remained loyal to God? God is not unjust as to punish the innocent with the guilty (2Pet.2:9). That is, God never destroyed these loyal Morning Stars along with their rebellious colleagues. Apparently, those loyal Morning Stars that were dwellers on earth would have been re-assigned to other parts of God's creation. Were they taken up to Heaven; are they the angels in Heaven right now? Or were they relocated to another planet(s) made conducive for their existence?

Where are these loyal Morning Stars today? We may not have the answers right now, but as we progress into eternity with God, when every form of sin and its consequences are permanently destroyed and settled eternally, the answers will definitely surface. We, who are the sons of God, will definitely re-join with these loyal Morning Stars, the Luciferic-age sons of God!

Boggling Questions

What this means is that there are many things we do not know yet. Many questions boggle the inquisitive mind of man, such as: Is there intelligent life out there outside the lives on earth and in Heaven? If there is, who are they? Are they the Luciferic Morning Stars that once dwelt on earth?

The Bible, the manual for man's existence, is very deep and full of information. Today, the Church, which is the only God's legal institution on earth, cannot claim to know all there is in Scriptures. Our knowledge of the Scriptures is increasing as the Spirit of God unveils to the Church per time. For instance, the first 1 500 years of its existence, the Church thought she knew all about the Scriptures. The Church taught that since man was the crown of God's glory, the earth where man dwelt was flat and it was the centre of the universe and all planetary bodies including the Sun moved around the earth. Scientists like Nicolaus Copernicus (AD 1473-1543) and Galileo Galilei (AD 1564-1642), who held different views, were ridiculed and even punished.

What a fallacy! That was human logic and not Scriptural at all. Such logic gave critics and atheists footholds to castigate the Bible.

However, it took several years of exploration and circum-navigation by men like Christopher Columbus (AD 1451-1506) and Ferdinand Magellan (AD 1480-1521) for humanity to accept that the earth is spherical. Notwithstanding, the Scriptures had categorically stated more than 3000 years before scientific confirmation and circumnavigation that the earth is spherical and rests on waters (Isa.40:22; Psa.24:1,2).

The implication of this is that the Scriptures are deep and coded in the language of God, and as we relate more and more with the Holy Spirit, our eyes will be opened more and more to see the reality of who we are in God. Indeed, what the Church knows today is far much more than what the first century Church knew; our knowledge of God and how He has created us are far greater than what Apostles Peter, Paul, etc. had. Because God used them to write the Scriptures does not mean that they knew all what they wrote; don't forget that they wrote not based on their knowledge but on the knowledge of the Author of life, the Holy Spirit (2Tim.3:16; 2Pet.1:20,21).

CHAPTER 13

THE SIGNIFICANCE OF LUCIFERIC JUDGMENT

THE WORLD OF LUCIFER, THE insurrection and the consequent judgment of the earth hold some significance to us today, and these are:

(1) THE AGE OF THE EARTH

Various archaeological researches have confirmed that the earth is far older than six thousand years as given by the Biblical account of the human age on earth (see BSS Book 4). As a result, many scholars think these archaeological findings did not correspond with the Biblical account of the age of humanity on earth. They, thus, conclude that the Bible is inaccurate in its account of creation. But a closer look at Biblical account shows no discrepancy whatsoever of the age of the earth. Humans were not the first dwellers on earth. The earth was not created at the same period man was created. The earth was created many years (possibly billions of years) before humans came on the scene. That was the Luciferic era.

Apparently, the earth was created at the time of Lucifer. It was a beautifully topographic scene. The earth was a chaste, artistic piece of divine mastery in its purity with a breath of perfection so much that the sons of God who were its dwellers 'shouted for joy' at its beauty. Indeed, the earth was a beautiful planet for its inhabitants, until Lucifer's insurrection started.

"Where were you [Job] when I established the earth?
Tell Me, if you have understanding.
Who fixed its dimensions? Certainly you know!
Who stretched a measuring line across it?
What supports its foundations?
Or who laid its cornerstone
while the morning stars sang together
and all the sons of God shouted for joy?" (Job 38:4-7 HCSB)

At this side of eternity, we may not know exactly how old the Earth was before it was destroyed due to Lucifer's rebellion. However, scientific discovery points to billions of years. This was based on the works of Marie Curie (1867-1934), Ernest Rutherford (1871-1937), and Arthur Holmes (1890-1964). In 1898, Marie Curie discovered the phenomenon of radioactivity, in which unstable atoms lose energy, or decay, by emitting radiation in the form of particles or electromagnetic waves, and by 1904 physicist Ernest Rutherford showed how this decay process could act as a clock for dating old rocks. In 1928, Arthur Holmes developed the technique of dating rocks using the radioactive isotopes of uranium-lead minerals.

As at today, the best estimate for earth's age has been made based on radiometric dating of fragments from the Canyon Diablo iron meteorite. From the fragments, radioactive uranium decay was calculated giving the estimated age of the earth to be about 3 billion years!

(2) PRE-HUMAN FOSSILS

Palaeontology or the study of fossils has constantly excavated pre-human bones and relics, some dating millions of years ago. These discoveries have made many scientific scholars to question the veracity of the Biblical account of creation. Some erroneously believe that the Biblical account of six thousand years of human existence contradict scientific discovery of pre-human fossil age of millions of years. But a closer study of the Bible shows no contradiction whatsoever in the creation account. As stated above, humans were not the first inhabitants of Planet Earth. Lucifer and the other sons of God inhabited earth for millions of years before the earth was destroyed by God due to Lucifer's rebellion.

During this Luciferic era, apparently, the Earth's population included millions of Morning Stars, animals and vegetation. The Morning Stars populated the earth, setting up kingdoms of nations with Lucifer as the overall leader. The Scriptures that referred to Lucifer and his fall in Ezekiel and Isaiah clearly state this fact.

"All the nations who knew you are appalled at you; you have come to a horrible end and will be no more" (Eze.28:19 NIV).

"Those who see you stare at you, they ponder your fate: Is this the man who shook the earth and made kingdoms tremble, the man who made the world a wilderness, who overthrew its cities and would not let his captives go home?" (Isa.14:16,17 NIV).

However, as discussed in Chapters 10 and 11, due to their rebellion, divine judgment came upon Lucifer and about one third of the dissident Morning Stars. One of the judgment was that they died physically and their bodies decomposed in the soil of the earth while their spirit lived on to become Satan and the demons. In addition, in order to wipe off all traces of the atrocities engendered by this rebellion from the surface of the earth, the earth was destroyed by God and covered with water. The animals, the vegetation and all other forms of life on earth were all destroyed.

Today's archaeological findings and paleontological discoveries are only unravelling the remains of this ancient world. Some dinosaurs and many other antiquated fossils of carbon-dated millions of years ago are all excavations of the bodies and remains of the Luciferic era.

As presented in chapter one, the oldest homo sapiens fossils to be discovered thus far are the bones of five different individuals excavated from an archaeological site, Jebel Irhoud, in Morocco of North Africa, and they were found to be about 300 000 years old. The facial features of the skulls look like a modern human, but the brain case is very elongated and archaically unlike ours. In other words, they look like us humans yet they were not exactly us. These are the remains of the dead bodies of the Morning Stars of the Luciferic era. Also, the microorganism vestiges dated to be at least 3770 million years old discovered in the Nuvvuagittuq Supracrustal Belt (NSB), Quebec, Canada (see chapter one) were the remains of the ancient Luciferic world.

Therefore, there should never be any misunderstanding or confusion of the Biblical truth on creation. The Bible is always and will be for ever true. God created all things; we are only now discovering what God had created. Unfortunately, the Church appears to be slow to catch up with science when it comes to such discoveries, thereby allowing erring scientists to give wrong interpretation of Biblical truths.

Today, the evolution theory has no strong scientific backing (see BSS Book 1), but because the Church is yet to discover the truth of the existence of Luciferic world, we have allowed the erroneous theory of evolution to persist. Luciferic world was true and existed before it was destroyed by God due to rebellion. This is in line with scientific discoveries of the age of the earth and the fossils.

(3) ORIGIN OF SIN

At the beginning of creation, all things were perfect; they functioned in perfect harmony as God desired them to be. But Lucifer, a created moral being with ability to make decisions, chose to disobey divine order, thereby sowing a seed of disharmony in God's creation. Soon, that disobedient thought infiltrated his whole being, resulting in full-blown rebellion, which attracted divine judgment. After being condemned, Lucifer became Satan and his once untainted nature became genetically reconfigured. His new genome that forms his new nature is what is now known as sin. That is the origin of sin.

Therefore, note the following truth:

- sin is simply the life of Satan
- sin started before the arrival of humans on earth
- sin is an antithesis of *zoe*; that is, the opposite of sin is *zoe*, the life of God.

THE NATURE OF SIN

The nature of sin is a stark opposite to the nature of zoe. Years later when Jesus arrived on earth, He further revealed the nature of sin; Jesus called Satan, the Devil. The term 'devil' is from the Greek word *diabolos*, which means 'a being proned to slander or false accusation.' Satan always seeks to slander the way of righteousness and accuses those that have the zoe nature.

In other words, *sin is the life of Satan, just as zoe is the life of God*. Putting it in scientific terms, all the genes that make up Satan are what is known as sin. Hence, sin-genome is the life of Satan. The sin-genome has characteristics by which its presence can be recognised or identified.

The characteristics of this sin nature of Satan are well articulated in Jesus' description of Satan:

> *"You are of your father, the devil, and it is your will to practice the lusts and gratify the desires [which are characteristic] of your father. He was a murderer from the beginning and does not stand in the truth, because there is no truth in him. When he speaks a falsehood, he speaks what is natural to him, for he is a liar [himself] and the father of lies and of all that is false"*
>
> *(Joh.8:44 AMP).*

John 8 verse 44 mentions three of the characteristics of sin – lust, murder and lying. Galatians 5 verses 19 to 21 mention additional 16 characteristics: adultery, fornication, impurity, lewdness, idolatry, sorcery, hatred, discord, jealousy, fits of rage, selfish ambition, dissensions, heresies, envy, drunkenness, and orgies. These and many others mentioned in the Scriptures are all characteristics or expressions of the sin-genome, the life of Satan. They all stand in complete opposite to the characteristics of zoe, the life of God.

THE BEGINNING OF RECREATION

CHAPTER 14
THE RECREATED EARTH

GOD'S ORIGINAL INTENTION FOR PLANET Earth and its galaxy was that the glory of God would cover the whole world. He created all things for His pleasure. God's pleasure is in the offering of praise and worship to Him. For this cause, He created all things.

> *"...the earth will be full of the knowledge of the Lord as the waters cover the sea" (Isa.11:9 AMP)*

> *"Thou art worthy, O Lord, to receive glory and honour and power: for thou hast created all things, and for thy pleasure they are and were created" (Rev.4:11 KJV).*

> *"Whoso offereth praise glorifieth me" (Psa.50:23 KJV)*

The Morning Stars, the sons of God on earth during the Luciferic era, were created to be part of the system that would bring God ultimate glory. Sin disrupted this divine plan. The result was that the earth was destroyed and covered with water. However, God's purpose had to be fulfilled. The counsel of God must stand. Divine plans cannot be thwarted (Pro.19:21; Num.23:19).

God, therefore, decided to restore the destroyed earth and recreate another set of Sons of God with the life of God (*zoe*) in them, who would fulfil His eternal purpose. How long the earth remained in utter destruction and covered with water and darkness following the Luciferic rebellion, we don't know. Most likely for thousands or millions of years!

"And the earth was without form, and void; and darkness was upon the face of the deep. And the Spirit of God moved upon the face of the waters" (Gen.1:2 KJV).

THE BEGINNING OF RECREATION

However, at the end, God started the restoration of the Earth. He began to call back those things that were destroyed. This was the beginning of the recreation of the world.

"And God said, Let there be light: and there was light. And God saw the light, that it was good: and God divided the light from the darkness. And God called the light Day, and the darkness he called Night. And the evening and the morning were the first day.

"And God said, Let there be a firmament in the midst of the waters, and let it divide the waters from the waters. And God made the firmament, and divided the waters which were under the firmament from the waters which were above the firmament: and it was so. And God called the firmament Heaven. And the evening and the morning were the second day.

"And God said, Let the waters under the heaven be gathered together unto one place, and let the dry land appear: and it was so. And God called the dry land Earth; and the gathering together of the waters called he Seas: and God saw that it was good.

"And God said, Let the earth bring forth grass, the herb yielding seed, and the fruit tree yielding fruit after his kind, whose seed is in itself, upon the earth: and it was so. And the earth brought forth grass, and herb yielding seed after his kind, and the tree yielding fruit, whose seed was in itself, after his kind: and God saw that it was good. And the evening and the morning were the third day.

"And God said, Let there be lights in the firmament of the heaven to divide the day from the night; and let them be for signs, and for seasons, and for days, and years: And let them be for lights in the firmament of the heaven to give light upon the earth: and it was so. And God made two great lights; the greater light to rule the day, and the lesser light to rule the night: he made the stars also. And God set them in the firmament of the heaven to give light upon the earth, and to rule over the day and over the night, and to divide the light from the darkness: and God saw that it was good. And the evening and the morning were the fourth day.

"And God said, Let the waters bring forth abundantly the moving creature that hath life, and fowl that may fly above the earth in the open firmament of heaven. And God created great whales, and every living creature that moveth, which the waters brought forth abundantly, after their kind, and every winged fowl after his kind: and God saw that it was good. And God blessed them, saying, Be fruitful, and multiply, and fill the waters in the seas, and let fowl multiply in the earth. And the evening and the morning were the fifth day.

"And God said, Let the earth bring forth the living creature after his kind, cattle, and creeping thing, and beast of the earth after his kind: and it was so. And God made the beast of the earth after his kind, and cattle after their kind, and everything that creepeth upon the earth after his kind: and God saw that it was good"

(Gen.1:3-25 KJV).

And so, by the 6th day of creation, God had restored the earth to its pre-Luciferic form, possibly with some additional embellishments. The earth again was teeming with living organisms – vegetation, fishes, birds, and land animals – with beautiful topographic landscapes, water bodies, and heavenly bodies such as stars, moons, asteroids, et cetera. Under divine inspiration, Apostle Peter succinctly documented the recreation story:

"For they deliberately overlook this fact, that the heavens existed long ago, and the earth was formed out of water and through water by the word of God" (2Pet.3:5 ESV).

The recreation of the earth was indeed a recreation. Since the earth was totally destroyed, God was more like creating it all over again. It was a massive reengineering and reconfiguration works. It was more like a write-off car from a ghastly accident, requiring massive reassembling and remodelling in order to get back its former shape and functions. Such an exercise can only be carried out by the manufacturer of the car and not by roadside mechanics and panel-beaters. In the same manner, God, the Manufacturer, took six full days to reassemble and remodel the destroyed earth in order to get back its former shape and functions. Indeed, it was a massive recreation that took six days!

Fig.11: Lucifer's act brought sin into the perfect creation. The result was that the earth was destroyed and covered with water by divine judgment. However, God's purpose of filling the earth with His glory had to be fulfilled. The counsel of God must stand. Divine plans cannot be thwarted. God, therefore, decided to restore the destroyed earth by calling out those things that were covered with water and darkness. *"And God said, Let there be light: and there was light,"* thus, marking the commencement of recreation of the destroyed earth!

THE MEANING OF SIX DAYS OF RECREATION

What exactly does the six days of recreation mean as mentioned in Genesis chapter one? Does it mean literal six days of our modern calendar or much more or less than the modern-calendar of six days?

Various Biblical scholars have given various calculations and submissions of what the six days of recreation mean. The most important consideration is that God is omnipotent. The human knowledge is too limited to appreciate and comprehend the vastness and magnitude of His power. The strength of bellowing waves and tornados, the supra-velocity of light, the energy potency of a uranium atom, the intensity of the black-holes in space, the dexterity of a moving shark, the unquantifiable heat of the earth's core, the vastness of the heavenlies, etc. are all but microscopic displays of the magnitude of divine power. In other words, God is more than able to recreate the entire earth in literal six days or even less. All it takes is to utter but a word from His mouth.

"Where the word of a king is, there is power" (Ecc.8:4 KJV)

"By faith we understand that the universe was created by the word of God, so that what is seen was not made out of things that are visible" (Heb.11:3 ESV).

On the other hand, could each recreated day represent a thousand years of human calendar, considering that a day is like a thousand years and a thousand years is like a day before God?

"But do not forget this one thing, dear friends: With the Lord a day is like a thousand years, and a thousand years are like a day"
(2Pet.3:8 NIV).

CHAPTER 15
THE ARRIVAL OF MAN

THE ULTIMATE PLAN OF GOD in recreating the world was to give birth to another species of sons of God who will reverberate the glory of God throughout the expanse of the universe, *"for the earth shall be filled with the knowledge of the glory of the Lord, as the waters cover the sea"* (Hab.2:14 KJV). That is, God was set to create another group of sons of God to repopulate the earth and who would replace the fallen Morning Stars.

To show the significance of this event, God put the creation of the new species of sons of God as the last event! Hence, after the entire universe was recreated, God then began the process of creating the new sons of God. This was done towards the end of the 6th day of recreation.

> *"And God said, Let us make man in our image, after our likeness: and let them have dominion over the fish of the sea, and over the fowl of the air, and over the cattle, and over all the earth, and over every creeping thing that creepeth upon the earth"*
>
> *(Gen.1:26 KJV).*

TO PORTRAY THE SIGNIFICANCE OF the event, for the first time since the recreation work had commenced, a solemn convocation of Trinity – the Father, Son and Holy Ghost – was called by God the Father to initiate the creation of the new species of sons of God. The eternal plan was to make new species that would look like God, beings that would have the same constituent characteristics as God. In other words, these beings would be sons of God with *zoe* flowing through them. God called these beings 'man' or mankind, also referred to as human beings or humanity.

THE THREE STAGES OF THE MAKING OF MAN

Note that the making of man by God was in three stages as follows:

(1) Creation of the human spirit

Genesis chapter one gives an account of the creation of the human spirit by God.

> *"So God created man in his own image, in the image of God created he him; male and female created he them" (Gen.1:27 KJV)*

God created human species, dividing them into two genders – male and female. The term 'create' is from the Hebrew word *'bara'* which means "to produce something from non-existing material substance." In other words, creation does not require the use of any physical material. As such, some authors define creation as 'producing something from nothing.' However, creation does not really mean producing something from nothing; this is because you still need a substance to create something, but that substance is non-materialistic. Non-materialistic refers to a thing or a substance that is NOT perceived by our five senses. This means non-materialistic substances are not earthly; they are something beyond physical existence.

God produced the human spirit from non-materialistic substance. The Bible clearly states that this non-materialistic substance used in creating the human spirit is the *God-substance*. That is, from His Spirit, God extracted material with which He used to produce the human spirit. In other words, the human spirit consists of the same materials that make up God. Concisely put, the human spirit and God's Spirit are made of the same materials. What makes God to be God is what was used to create the human spirit (for more of this, see SSB Book 1).

After God created the human spirits, He blessed them.

> *"So God created man in his own image, in the image of God created he him; male and female created he them. And God blessed them, and God said unto them..." (Gen.1:27,28 KJV).*

That is how God had completed His recreation; the human spirits were the last to be created on the sixth day. No other works of creation occurred after the making of the human spirits on the sixth day. In other words, humans are the epitome, the grand finale, of God's creation. Man is the masterpiece of God's design.

The next day, the seventh day, was a day of rest. That is, God rested on the seventh day after finishing His work of creation on the sixth day, thereby setting a divine order for man, which is rest comes after work and not the other way round; laziness is resting before working, which is the reverse of divine order.

> *"Thus the heavens and the earth were finished, and all the host of them. And on the seventh day God ended his work which he had made; and he rested on the seventh day from all his work which he had made" (Gen.2:1,2 KJV).*

(2) The Formation of the Human Body

After God rested on the seventh day, an interesting thing He did was the formation of the human body. The Bible did not specifically state which day the event occurred. However, we know that this event occurred after the seventh day of rest, possibly many days after creation had ended.

"And the LORD God formed [yatsar] man of the dust of the ground, and breathed into his nostrils the breath of life; and man became a living soul" (Gen.2:7 KJV).

Note that the Bible did not mince any words or make any mistake in stating the formation of the human body. According to Genesis chapter 2 verse 7, the human body was FORMED and NOT CREATED. The term 'form' in that Scripture is from the Hebrew word *'yatsar,'* which means 'to fashion or frame something into a certain shape using a material substance.' In other words, the human body was fashioned or framed into a specific shape using material from the earth. Indeed, that material is the soil or dust of the earth as clearly translated by Contemporary English Version:

> *"The Lord God took a handful of soil and made a man" (Gen.2:7 CEV).*

Indeed, we should never confuse the events of Genesis chapters one and two. In chapter one God created the human spirits while in chapter two He formed the human body. He picked soil and moulded it into a shape like His. Obviously, the moulded shape was patterned after the created human spirit, which is in turn patterned after the shape or image of God. Therefore, humans bear the shape of God.

That is how the human body was formed. The angels gaze at such a beautiful edifice. Satan and the demons were stupefied as they were confused about what the Omniscient meant to do. None knew the mind of the Master as He went about His moulding meticulously with ultra-rapt attention.

(3) The Union of the Human spirit and the Human Body

Finally, the moulding was finished. What an artistic beauty! A true reflection of divine purity! God stepped back, took a good appraisal of His work. And behold it was good! 'Good' means perfect. It means unfathomably exquisite beauty that cannot be accurately articulated in human words. The angels and demons gasped with surprise!

Then God did an amazing thing! He took the moulded image and from His nostrils He exhaled into the nostrils of the moulded image.

> *"And the LORD God formed man of the dust of the ground, and breathed into his nostrils the breath of life...." (Gen.2:7 KJV).*

But it was not just ordinary expiration. It was not that God was exhausted and had to catch a breath or His nose was blocked by particles of dust and had to exhale out the obstruction. Rather, this was a life-giving breath. The Bible calls it the 'breath of life.' The literal meaning of this phrase is 'spirit of life.' The 'breath' in that phrase is the Hebrew word '*neshama*,' which means 'spirit.' It means God breathed a 'spirit of life' into the moulded image.

As discussed earlier, the human spirits had been already created on the sixth day of Creation and were existing in God. Thus, God took one of these human spirits and injected it into the moulded image. He injected the created human spirit through His nose into the nostrils of the moulded image via the process of breathing. In other words, God breathed one of the created human spirits into the moulded image. Consequently, the human spirit left the inside of God and became deposited in the moulded image.

Once this occurred, an amazing thing happened – the moulded image suddenly came alive! The moulded eyelids could move, exposing the hidden spirit that is living in the inside. The moulded image could talk, walk, run, et cetera. The angels, Satan and demons were aghast with words! They watched as this newly arrived being on earth came alive and started engaging in intellectual discourse with the Almighty. The moulded image was no longer an 'it,' but a 'he.' He has life and could respond to his environment intellectually. In other words, the human spirit that entered the moulded image brought life to the moulded image. And so, life was not from the body but from the human spirit.

> *"And the LORD God formed man of the dust of the ground, and breathed into his nostrils the breath of life; and man became a living soul" (Gen.2:7 KJV).*

> *"...the body without the spirit is dead" (Jam.2:26 KJV).*

"It is the spirit that giveth life; the flesh profiteth nothing"

(Joh.6:63 ASV).

The angels burst out in songs of admiration, adoration and worship of the wisdom of the Ancient in bringing to life such a beautiful masterpiece of creation. God called this new arrival *Adam*, which means 'mankind.' He is much like his Father, God; the life of God (*zoe*) flowed expressly through him. He was another species of the sons of God:

"...Adam, the son of God" (Luk.3:38 KJV).

Fig.12: *"And the Lord God formed man of the dust of the ground, and breathed into his nostrils the breath of life; and man became a living being.......So God created man in His own image; in the image of God He created him"* (Gen.2:7; 1:27,28 NKJV).

Chapter 16

The Dominion Mandate of Man

Man was created in the image and likeness of God. The first man to appear on earth was named Adam, which means mankind. He carried *zoe*, the life of God, in him. He was a son of God.

> *"Adam was the son of God" (Luke 3:38 NLT)*

> *"Adam's father was God" (Luke 3:38 TLB).*

Man was given the authority of rulership (dominion) over the new earth, the very same authority that Lucifer abused. He was to perpetuate the praise and worship of God on earth. In other words, like Lucifer, man was to establish divine order on earth as it is in Heaven.

Man's dominion over the earth is in four dimensions. These four dimensions constitute the legitimate divine authority of man on earth; that is the **Divine Quadrupled Dominion Mandate (DQDM)** of man, refers to simply as the **Dominion Mandate**:

(1) FRUITFULNESS

Man was not created barren. He was to bear fruits. He had the capability of reproduction. Like all other creatures, God put seed in a man for this purpose of reproduction. That is, reproduction is only possible by the presence of seed.

Reproduction does not only mean biological, but also includes every other endeavour. Man had been inbuilt with the ability to generate seed-thought (idea), which when sown could grow into plants (products) that would produce fruits. In short, failure was never part of man's original nature.

(2) MULTIPLICATION

Not only would man be fruitful, he also had the capability to double, triple, etc. his fruits. That is, after bearing fruits, man could multiply his fruits on earth. Multiplication is not limited to biological, but in all areas of endeavours. In other words, once his idea has borne fruit, man has the inherent ability to multiply the fruit around his world.

(3) REPLENISHMENT

This refers to the ability of continuous refilling or replacement. It denotes the state of continual renewal. That is, not only would man be fruitful and multiply, but he also had the capability of refilling, replacing, and renewing the earth with his multiplied fruits. In other words, man was inbuilt with the capability of filling the earth with all sorts of fruits. He was not to bring out and multiply only one type of fruits. He had an innate ability to produce varieties of fruits and keep replacing them as the needs arose. This would bring beauty and colour to the earth, just as it is in Heaven. God is a Being of variety and He had created man to be like Himself.

(4) SUBDUE

This refers to the ability to bring under control or to subjugate under an authority. Man was given the divine ability to subjugate the whole world under his authority. By this ability, nothing should lord over man. Through his seed-thoughts (ideas), he is to bear fruits, which should multiply and replenish the earth, and finally conquer the earth.

Important Lesson!

The important lesson here is that any idea you have is expected by God to become fruitful, and then to multiply, replenish, and conquer its field. Nothing living or non-living on earth should be able to conquer you. Mosquitoes were not permitted to bring malaria that would subdue and kill man. In the same vein, no sickness, disease, ill-luck, bad-luck, misfortune was to conquer man. There was no natural disaster, mental disability, or spiritual force that had the power to subjugate man under its control. Man was made to be the lord of all; he was only answerable to his Maker. This was the original divine plan for man; it's a plan of total dominion of the earth for the worship of the Creator God.

In simple words, man was made a 'god' on earth. Nothing could happen on earth without his permission. No being, be it angel, Satan, or demons, was permitted to lord over man on earth. The earth is man's home and his plenipotentiary jurisdiction. The only Person man was answerable to was his Father, God.

*"So God created man in his own image, in the image of God created he him; male and female created he them. And God blessed them, and God said unto them, '**Be fruitful**, and **multiply**, and **replenish** the earth, and **subdue** it: and have dominion over the fish of the sea, and over the fowl of the air, and over every living thing that moveth upon the earth. And God said, Behold, I have given you every herb bearing seed, which is upon the face of all the earth, and every tree, in the which is the fruit of a tree yielding seed; to you it shall be for meat. And to every beast of the earth, and to every fowl of the air, and to everything that creepeth upon the earth, wherein there is life, I have given every green herb for meat: and it was so" Gen.1:27-30 KJV).*

THE CAPABILITY FOR TRANSFORMATION

Man's Dominion Mandate never made one man to subjugate another man. Man was not created to conquer and subdue his fellow man; rather his mandate was over the animals, vegetation and elements of his world. By his divine mandate, man was inbuilt with the capability of transforming his world into a beautiful Paradise; he was to transform the earth to be like Heaven, where the Throne of God is situated. As such, God planted a Garden of Eden as an example of the eternal divine plan for man.

Therefore, slavery, colonialism, fascism, racism, and all other forms of subjugation were originally foreign to the nature of man; they were seen in man after his Fall. That is, man was created with the capability for transformation of his world and not for subjugating his fellow man.

THE EXPANSE OF MAN'S AUTHORITY

The sky provides layers of space that harbours the stars and moon that provides light on earth. Hence, the sky exists because of the earth. Note that since the sky exists because of the earth, man's authority also extends to the sky.

> *"And God said, Let there be lights in the firmament of the heaven to divide the day from the night; and let them be for signs, and for seasons, and for days, and years: And let them be for lights in the firmament of the heaven to give light upon the earth: and it was so. And God made two great lights; the greater light to rule the day, and the lesser light to rule the night: he made the stars also. And God set them in the firmament of the heaven to give light upon the earth, and to rule over the day and over the night, and to divide the light from the darkness: and God saw that it was good. And the evening and the morning were the fourth day"*
>
> *(Gen.1:14-19 KJV).*

FIRST EXERCISE OF THE DOMINION MANDATE

As a confirmation of his Dominion Mandate over the earth, man executed two projects immediately he arrived on earth:

(1) Cultivation of the Earth

> *"The Lord God put the man in the Garden of Eden to take care of it and to look after it" (Gen.2:15 CEV)*

Adam's divine commission was to 'tend and dress' (Gen.2:15 KJV) his home, the Garden of Eden. That is, he was "to take care of it and to look after it." The earth was full of raw materials, and Adam and his offspring were to use their ability to beautify the entire earth for their comfortable habitation, starting from the Garden of Eden. He was given divine authority to execute this assignment. The process for achieving such a feat is work. Adam was commissioned to work by the God who made him. In other words, work is a divine assignment and not a man-made formulation!

The Three Characteristics of Work

There are three characteristics of this divine assignment, work, given to Adam:

a) Work was to Enforce the Dominion Mandate
Work is the divine design meant to beautify the earth and enrich man's life. Adam's work was to make him fruitful, multiply, replenish and subdue the earth. That is, the Dominion Mandate of fruitfulness, multiplication, replenishment and subduing of the earth can only be realised via the process of work. For that reason, without work, man cannot become fruitful, multiply, replenish and subdue the earth.

b) Work made Adam Co-Creator

Adam's spirit, soul and body were inbuilt with the divine creative capability to fulfil the divine fourfold Dominion Mandate of fruitfulness, multiplication, replenishment and subduing of the earth. However, it would be through the work process that such creative capability would be unleashed. In other words, work was to make Adam a co-creator with divinity.

Through work, Adam and his offspring would be able to transform the raw earth into an exquisite Paradise, starting from the Garden of Eden. Through work, God expected Adam and his progenies to turn the trees into buildings, the sand into glasses, the earth elements into microchips, and so on. God has inbuilt Man with creative ability just like the Creator Himself, hence, he was to convert the waves of the rivers into electrical energy and all other forms of energy, the silicon element of the earth into transmitters for effective communication, the gold of Ophir and Havilah into beautiful structural designs for data storage, and the diamonds of Rhodesia into ornamental products.

God gave Man a prudent heart and a discerning mind to methodological structure his world and segment it into operational data. Man has the ability to transform the lightning of the thunder into high-speed transportation system to explore his world and the galaxies, the radiations of the Sun into abundant energy that should power his agriculture and all his industries, et cetera. In other words, Man was infinite in creative ingenuity just as his Father God, who never created him to be destitute – *poverty, ignorance,* and *diseases*, the three greatest enemies of man, were never part of his original nature.

c) Work was to be a productive venture

Work was not designed by the Father to punish his son, Adam. Rather, his Father designed work to engage Adam and make him productive. Adam's work was to yield dividends. It was impossible for Adam to work and not see the commensurate results. Working without productivity is a curse. In simple term, work was to be a blessing and not a curse! That is, Adam's work was abundantly blessed to be productive; his work was never to be a curse. Work was not a curse in the original divine design.

In summary
Adam was not expected to be idle and do nothing. Doing nothing is idleness, which is laziness. That is, laziness is the opposite of work, and Adam was commissioned to work and not be lazy. Laziness would bring boredom. But Adam's life was far from being bored. He moved about his new home, supervising the animals and tending the fields. As he progressed, he would enter the realm of scientific and technological breakthroughs.

Definitely, Adam's life was never a boring one. I believe Adam could fly across the earth and into the sky supervising his home, swim into the depths of the ocean, walk on waters, pass through material walls easily, and he possessed far superior intelligence than the present mankind on earth. The second and last Adam, Jesus Christ (1Cor.15:45), did all these things while He walked on earth, invariably letting us to know that was how the Father originally created mankind.

(2) Giving of Names

To be fully in charge of his home, earth, Adam had to identify all the things in it. He did this by attaching a name to everything in his dominion. Thus, Adam gave names to everything on earth. By doing that, Adam was simply expressing his Dominion Mandate. To show the authority of man over the earth, any name Adam gave was never disapproved by God. Any name Adam gave to anything was permanent on earth and in Heaven. In other words, any name given by man on earth is recognised in Heaven.

> *"So the Lord God formed out of the ground every wild animal and every bird of the sky, and brought each to the man to see what he would call it. And whatever the man called a living creature, that was its name. The man gave names to all the livestock, to the birds of the sky, and to every wild animal..." (Gen.2:19,20 HCSB)*

It is better to pause at this stage and consider the full import of name-giving. What if there were no names? Communication would become clumsy and seed-thoughts (ideas) would not be effectively cultivated to yield fruits. In other words, productivity is clearly linked to name-giving. Adam's creative vision and goals would need to be communicated in clear names to his offspring for them to become fruitful. That is, name-giving was an expression of man's divine Dominion Mandate of fruitfulness, multiplication, replenishment, and subdue of the earth.

CHAPTER 17
MAN – A SOCIAL BEING

ADAM WAS THE ONLY HUMAN being in the whole world. No other human was there with him. How long Adam lived alone without any other human, the Scriptures were silent; apparently for years! He soon started feeling lonely. The animals that he named could not fill in the vacuum of loneliness. He was created a social being, and he needed a social interaction that is superior to what he had with the animals in Eden.

> *"And the LORD God said, It is not good that the man should be alone; I will make him an help meet for him. And out of the ground the LORD God formed every beast of the field, and every fowl of the air; and brought them unto Adam to see what he would call them: and whatsoever Adam called every living creature, that was the name thereof. And Adam gave names to all cattle, and to the fowl of the air, and to every beast of the field; but for Adam there was not found an help meet for him"* (Gen.2:18-20 KJV).

The term 'helpmeet' in Genesis chapter 2 verses 18 to 20 (KJV) is from the Hebrew word *ezer*, which means 'helper or succour.' CEV translates it as 'partner.' In other words, the vacuum of loneliness in Adam could only be filled by a partner. Partners are mates or companions of same kind. Animals are of different kind of species, hence, they do not have the same life as humans even though some of them like the apes may somewhat have similar shapes. An angel or any other being could not become Adam's partner because they are different kind of beings from mankind.

Indeed, Adam knew he had a need but might not have known what exactly would satisfy that need. But God who created man knew exactly what could satisfy that lonely desire of Adam. Adam was alone and lonely and needed a mankind partner.

THE FIRST HUMAN SURGERY

To satisfy Adam's need, God gave the first general anaesthesia to Adam. He put Adam into a deep sleep. While he was under the effect of the general anaesthesia, God performed the first surgery on human body. He took one of the ribs of Adam and with it, He produced a female species of mankind.

"So the Lord God made him fall into a deep sleep, and he took out one of the man's ribs. Then after closing the man's side, the Lord made a woman out of the rib" (Gen.2:21 CEV).

Some people do wonder how a small rib could be utilised to form a whole human body! But science has shown that it is very possible. To produce the female body from the rib of Adam, God might have first crushed the excised rib into powder to obtain the various component elements. Thereafter, God would have amplified the rib powder, a process much like the polymerase chain reaction of biological elements such as the deoxyribonucleic acid (DNA). After He had amplified the rib powder into the quantity He needed, God then meticulously moulded the rib powder into the shape of a woman.

When the moulding was completed, behold it was exquisitely beautiful, a perfection of beauty! Next, God would have taken one of the created human spirits that resided in Him, and breathed the spirit into the nostrils of the moulded body. Immediately the human spirit entered into the moulded body, the body came alive. Thus, a female species of mankind had been formed.

The Significance of the Rib Choice

Why the rib? Why not another part of the human body? The significance of choosing the rib is astonishing. The all-wise God knew what He was doing.

The reason He chose to make this female species of mankind from the man's rib can be adduced from the functions of a rib, which include:

• Protective Function
The ribcage protects three vital organs in the body – a heart and two lungs. These organs are vital for the human body survival, and the ribcage provides the necessary protective coverage for them.

• Respiratory Function
The ribcage aids in respiration, which is vital for energy production and excretion of toxic wastes like carbon dioxide. In other words, without respiration, the body dies, and the ribs ensure the success of the respiratory process.

• Productive Function
The ribs are essential part of the system that produces blood in the body by a process called *hematopoiesis*. Blood is essential for life; the ribs, therefore, guarantee the human body survival.

Indeed, the importance of the rib to human existence is unquestionable. Without the ribs, the human body would be dysfunctional and would be unable to survive successfully on earth. It was from a rib that God made the body of the female mankind.

In other words, God is letting mankind to know that without the female species, man's capability to survive on earth will be unattainable and impracticable. That is, man would become extinct without a woman. This means that a male-male relationship or a female-female relationship is unnatural; such an unnatural relationship will ultimately result in the extinction of the human race. In other words, homosexuality is never the original plan of the Creator; it is an invention from Satan, the enemy of man.

> *"So God created man in his own image, in the image of God created he him; male and female created he them" (Gen.1:27 KJV).*

> *"But from the beginning of the creation God made them male and female" (Mar.10:6 KJV).*

THE FIRST DIVINE INSTITUTION ON EARTH

Interestingly, after the female species of mankind had been produced by God, two things happened:

(1) God Himself brought the female species to the man

God did not allow the female species to be discovered by Adam or wait for her to introduce herself to Adam. God Himself brought the female specie to the man, Adam.

> *"The Lord God brought her to the man" (Gen.2:22 CEV)*

The term 'brought' in Genesis chapter 2 verse 22 is from the Hebrew word *bow*, which means "to go in, enter, or come in." In other words, this was not just an ordinary introduction of the female species to the man. It was the divine union of the man and the female species. That is, the female 'entered into,' 'went into,' or 'came into' a divine relationship with the man. This was a holy matrimony; a divine relationship that we now call marriage.

In other words, a marriage was conducted by God between Adam and the female. That is, marriage is an institution established by God between a man and a woman. Therefore, marriage involves three persons: a man, a woman, and God. Marriage is a union of a man and a woman with God linking the man and the woman together. Marriage is *"a threefold cord [that] is not quickly broken"* (Ecc.4:12 NKJV). What this means is: in the eyes of Divinity, without these three persons (man, woman, and God) being present, any relationship can never be a marriage. Thus, marriage is defined as the union of a man and a woman by God.

(2) Adam received the Female Specie

The anaesthetic effect waned off after the divine surgery and Adam woke up. Then God 'brought' the female species to Adam in a marital union. Immediately, Adam sighted the female species at his side, he knew this species came from him and was the true companion that could fill in his loneliness. He excitedly exclaimed:

> *"And Adam said, This is now bone of my bones, and flesh of my flesh: she shall be called Woman, because she was taken out of Man. Therefore shall a man leave his father and his mother, and shall cleave unto his wife: and they shall be one flesh"*
>
> *(Gen.2:23,24 KJV).*

> *"The Lord God brought her to the man, and the man exclaimed: 'Here is someone like me! She is part of my body, my own flesh and bones. She came from me, a man. So I will name her Woman!'"*
> *(Gen.2:23,24 CEV).*

Thus, Adam knew beyond any shadow of doubt that the female species was not from a gorilla or chimpanzee family nor from an angelic realm, but truly from him. Immediately, he (Adam) proceeded to name the female species **'woman,'** which is from the Greek word **'ishshah'** that means **'female species of mankind.'**

The question, therefore, is: *how did Adam know she came from him?* The Bible did not mention how Adam came to know that the female species came from him. But we must realise that Adam was primarily a spirit being that had a soul and lived in a physical body. Obviously, his spirit picked the information from God. The eido centre of Adam's spirit picked the information from God that the female species was from him, and hence, he called her 'woman.'

Another significant point of consideration was that Adam felt completely at peace with the woman at his side. That is, he felt totally at home with her. This is evident in his speech, which clearly shows that Adam fully accepted the woman she saw at his side as he woke up from the sedative effect of the anaesthesia. In other words, there was a mutual acceptance of the man and the woman. This is of great importance in man's decision-making, especially, a decision as crucial as choice of marital spouse. When you come in contact with what God has for you, there is always a peaceful tranquillity that fills your heart; in such situation, your heart becomes flooded with peace, quietness and confidence, which was what Adam and the woman felt about each other as they were brought into a marital union by their Father, God.

Fig.13: From one of the ribs of Adam, God made a female companion, Eve, for the man, and then joined the man and the woman in holy matrimony in their exquisitely beautiful home, the Garden of Eden. *"God blessed them, and God said to them, 'Be fruitful and multiply; fill the earth and subdue it; have dominion over the fish of the sea, over the birds of the air, and over every living thing that moves on the earth'"* (Gen.1:28 NKJV).

Chapter 18

The Intense Hatred of Satan Against Humans

Meanwhile, many eyes were watching the unfolding events on the recreated earth. The angels gasped with utter astonishment at the wisdom of the Ancient as they saw the unfolding magnificence of Adam and his wife in their splendid home, the Garden of Eden.

THE GARDEN OF EDEN

God, being a good Father, built a beautiful home, the Garden of Eden, for the first human couple to dwell in and to continually improve upon its glory to their taste (Gen.2:15). Eden was a Paradise of exquisite tranquillity and beauty, unrivalled anywhere in the whole of the recreated world. It had all manner of lovely flowers, shrubs, trees, animals, and a crystal clear river that parted into four riverheads running through it.

The radiant glory of the firmament was visible skywards pouring rays of love and joy into Adam's home with, above all, the Presence of Divinity, bathing and encircling the whole arena. Adam and Eve, with their animals, revelled in this gorgeous home of glory. The Garden of Eden was built by Father, God, Himself specifically for the comfort and joy of the new couple. Eden is a Hebrew word that means 'pleasure.' Since God names things for their attributes, the Garden of Eden was a home for exquisite pleasures far unfathomed and incomprehensible by our present natural senses.

"The Lord God planted a garden eastward in Eden, and there He put the man whom He had formed. And out of the ground the Lord God made every tree grow that is pleasant to the sight and good for food. The tree of life was also in the midst of the garden, and the tree of the knowledge of good and evil. Now a river went out of Eden to water the garden, and from there it parted and became four riverheads" (Gen.2: 8-10 NKJV)

As a tale of its paragon of beauty, God also made precious metals and stones and kept them in the land of Havilah. Such metals include nuggets of pure gold and beautiful bdellium, and lapis lazuli (onyx stones).

"The name of the first [riverhead] is Pishon; it is the one which skirts the whole land of Havilah, where there is gold. And the gold of that land is good. Bdellium and the onyx stone are there" (Gen.2:11,12 NKJV).

These metals and stones did not grow on trees, but where located within the soil or crevices of mountains. In order words, in His divine wisdom, God 'concealed' the precious metals and beautiful stones for man to discover. Imagine the pleasant surprise, the ecstasy, which Adam and Eve must have experienced as they roamed about their home to discover these precious beauties! As their minds grew and developed, they would have reached a state where they would have started converting these precious substances into other invaluable uses. In order words, life in the Garden of Eden was never boring as there were a lot to do to keep Adam and Eve busy.

THE PRETENSION OF SATAN

Also watching the unfolding events on the recreated earth were Satan and his demons. As the events unfolded, Satan and his demons read the implied meanings into what the Almighty was doing, and were enraged beyond measures. They hated not just God, but His works. They hated man, his marriage, and his new world with such unqualified passion.

Indeed, many people who have had contact with Satan and demons often wonder why they hate humans with such great passion. Most havocs, diseases, disasters, miseries, heartaches, et cetera are direct effects of demonic antagonisms. Most family breakages that destroy children's lives, poverty, and untold ignorance are fingers of demons at work.

Satan and demons may pretend to be good and nice to a man, but once they succeed in getting what they want from him, they finally reveal and vent their true hatred on him. The pathetic state of the man at the tomb that was possessed with several demons (Mar.5:1-13) in AD 32 is a good example. The man's life was in total disarray because of the wickedness of the demons that possessed his body. Judas Iscariot, one of the disciples of Jesus, was a trusted disciple, a good man, until Satan entered into him and wreaked havoc in his life, finally leading to his suicide and eternal perishing in Hell (Luk.22:3, Mat.27:3-5).

It is of great significance to always remember that Satan and his demons are no longer angelic Lucifer and Morning Stars. Their nature has been irredeemably changed and reconfigured to form evil. They are evil personified, hence, their descriptive names, *'evil spirits.'* As evil spirits, they lack the capacity for mercy or remorse. They enjoy inflicting suffering on man and are jubilant when humans wallow in misery. Never doubt this. It is sheer stupidity for any human to sell himself to any of these evil spirits as it is becoming a common practice these days. The hatred of these evil spirits against humans often baffles people who witness such hatred in its raw form.

TWO REASONS WHY SATAN AND DEMONS HATE HUMANS

But why do Satan and demons hate humans with such an intense passion that defiles human understanding? Why are they ready to steal, kill and ultimately destroy once they have the slightest opportunity?

"The thief [evil spirit] comes only to steal and kill and destroy..."
(Joh.10:10 RSV).

There are two reasons why these evil spirits, Satan and his demons, hate humans with such an intense, undying passion:

(a) Humans are Arch-Rivals

Humans were made to replace what Lucifer and his Morning Stars (now Satan and the demons respectively) had lost. We have been made in the image and likeness of God, and commissioned to re-establish the divine harmony that the Luciferic era had distorted.

Adam was created in the image and likeness of God to be a 'god' on earth, the very same role that was once assigned to Lucifer. Satan (the fallen Lucifer) and his demons saw this and became enraged with jealousy and anger. Hence, they see humans as rivals and sworn enemies that must be defeated and conquered and his assigned divine role frustrated.

(b) The Great Conflict between Good and Evil

By conquering humans, Satan believes he is scoring a point against God, and which is to perpetually frustrate the divine plan of achieving a perfect harmonious creation that will worship the Father of Glory, the Creator of the universe, forever and ever. Fallen Lucifer, who became Satan, still entertains delusional thoughts that he can somewhat succeed in his evil plot. Satan knows of his approaching end in the Lake of Fire, but thinks he can still thwart his doom by scuttling divine plan. As such, he relentlessly launches frantic and frenzy battles against divine plan at any slightest opportunity.

It is the conflicting war between the forces of good and evil; a war of spirits that far transcends our physical existence and the natural world! It is the Great Conflict between Good and Evil. Thus, immediately man arrived on earth, Satan started plotting a device to counter this new divine order.

THE FALL OF HUMANITY

CHAPTER 19
THE FALL OF MAN

THUS, THE WORK OF RECREATING the destroyed earth had been completed. Thereafter, God made the first human, Adam, and later joined him in holy matrimony with his wife, whom Adam later named Eve, which means *"the mother of all living"* (Gen.3:20 KJV). By joining Adam and Eve in holy matrimony, God has established a new institution, the *Marriage Institution*, also known as the *Family*.

Through the family units, the purpose of God would be established on earth. As stated earlier, the purpose of God has been that the glory of God would fill the whole earth and its galaxies as it is in Heaven, which is where the Throne of God is situated. Luciferic beings failed in this assignment, hence, humanity was formed to execute that divine purpose.

While Adam and Eve were revelling in their new home, the Garden of Eden, Satan and his demons were languishing in their condemned state in Hell. The spiritual world is as real as the physical world of earth, and distance is not a restriction in the spiritual world. Hence, Satan and his demons watched with keen interest how the new species of mankind were blissfully gliding around the earth in their innocence. Satan and his demons could see that humanity had been created to replace them and execute divine purpose on earth. They knew Adam and his wife had been inbuilt with the potential and granted such authority to fulfil the divine purpose.

Therefore, with such envy and loathsome hatred, Satan called for a meeting with his demons, and they resolved never to allow this divine plan to become fruitful. Interestingly, despite his fall and divine judgment, Satan, who was a former angel Lucifer, still delusionally believed he could scheme his way through and realise his evil intention of dethroning God and establishing his rule over the universe. He, therefore, began another session of evil plot, which was another round of Conflict of Good and Evil.

THE TREE OF THE KNOWLEDGE OF GOOD AND EVIL

Meanwhile, in the home, the Garden of Eden, built for Adam and his wife, Eve, God planted two trees of great significance:
    (a) the Tree of the Knowledge of Good and Evil (Gen.2:15-17)
    (b) the Tree of Life (Gen.3:24)

For the Tree of the Knowledge of Good and Evil, God laid out instructions (also known as regulations, laws, or commandments) for Adam and his wife to follow:

> *"The Lord God took the man and put him in the Garden of Eden to work it and take care of it. And the Lord God commanded the man, 'You are free to eat from any tree in the garden; but you must not eat from the tree of the knowledge of good and evil, for when you eat from it you will certainly die'" (Gen.2:15-17 NIV).*

The disturbing questions are: Why would God plant the Tree of the Knowledge of Good and Evil? Why would God give the commandment of not eating the fruit of this tree? Didn't He know Satan would take advantage of such a law to wreak havoc in the human family? Didn't God know Adam and his wife would fall to the wicked scheme of Satan?

The answer to these questions is yes. God's omniscience knew that Satan would take advantage of such a commandment and wreak havoc in the human family, and He knew Adam and his wife would fall to the wicked scheme of Satan. Yes, Father God knew all this, and yet He planted the tree and gave the commandment due to the following reasons:

(i) Fulfilment of divine purpose

God is a God of orderliness and purpose (1Cor.14:40 KJV). To maintain an order requires regulations or laws, which are also known commandments. The absence of a law breeds chaos, which is the opposite of orderliness. For Adam and his progeny to realise the purpose of their creation, they would have to follow stipulated requirements. Thus, the commandment of God was given to them to maintain orderliness while pursuing the divine mandate. Obeying the divine commandment would help in the smooth running of their home and, hence, fulfilling the divine agenda for their lives.

(ii) Protection of the young human family

Satan had not yet been permanently confined to the Lake of Fire; he still had the privilege of roaming about, accessing the recreated world from his condemned home, Hell. Hence, he could come up to the recreated earth, and move to and fro across it (Job 1:6,7; 2:1,2). God knew this, and being a good Father, He wanted to protect the young human family from the evil manipulations of Satan and the demons. Like any earthly father who protects his children from the wickedness in the land, so also God was protecting His children, Adam and Eve.

Every living thing God creates grows. Growth is one of the characteristics of living organisms. In the same way, Adam and his wife, Eve, were to grow in stature, strength and wisdom. The fruits from the Tree of the Knowledge of Good and Evil were one mechanism of increasing man's levels of wisdom. One such level of wisdom is to have full knowledge of good and evil. Attaining such knowledge comes with responsibility, which is the ability to choose good over evil. Like children, Adam and Eve appeared not yet fully mature to comprehend and ward off the evils of Satan. Their wisdom was still growing. As children, their strength and wisdom had not yet reached such a level to be able to fully resist the full weight of evil and chose good. If they chose evil (sin), the nature of Satan, the Law of Death would kick in and they would die. As a result, God gave them such a commandment not to eat the fruits from the Tree of Knowledge of Good and Evil in order to protect them from death and eternal destruction. Oh what fatherly care!

God Never Tempts Anyone

God would not just plant a tree of attraction like the Tree of Knowledge of Good and Evil in the midst of the Garden as a means of tempting mankind. God does not tempt anyone (Jam.1:13). God can, and does, test His children, like He did unto Abraham (Gen. chpt. 22) and King Hezekiah (2Chr.32:31).

To tempt is to try an individual with the intention of making him fall into harm while to test is to try an individual with the intention of promoting him to next level. For instance, the aim of conducting a school test or exam is to promote a student to next level. That is, the target of temptation is demotion while the target of testing is promotion. Satan tempts while God tests. The commandment about the fruits of the Tree of Knowledge of Good and Evil is a test and not a temptation for Adam and his wife. By obeying God, they would grow in their love, strength, and wisdom in the quest for fulfilling their divine assignment.

It appears that when they, Adam and his wife, Eve, would have grown to a point of full responsibility of deciding good for evil, God would have then permitted them to eat the fruits of the Tree of Knowledge of Good and Evil. However, at the moment, the commandment was for them to avoid the fruits.

The Sinister Plot

As his nature has been, Satan wandered into the Garden of Eden, the home of Adam and Eve. He had an ulterior motive, which was to execute his evil plot to counter and annul the plan of God for humanity.

Satan knew the enormity of authority wielded by the humans (Adam and Eve) over the entire earth, which was their jurisdiction. Satan's strength wouldn't match such enormous authority. Therefore, he cunningly devised a strategy to disarm these innocently growing humans, who apparently were yet to be fully matured into their inheritance of power and wisdom. Adam and Eve were like toddlers, who were still crawling even though they have the full human potential of walking at the appropriate age. That is, though Adam and Eve had all the authority and wisdom in their disposition to be the lords of their home, planet earth, yet like toddlers they would need to grow into that inheritance. The Commandment of God forbidding them from eating the fruits from the Tree of Knowledge of Good and Evil was to protect them from satanic evil, while they grew and matured into their inheritance of power and wisdom; just like a good father would protect his growing children so was Father God protecting these growing humans by issuing such a commandment.

Wouldn't it be better if God had created Adam and his wife, Eve, as fully grown and well-matured adults that would not need any such protection and tender care? If God did that, it would have negated the principle of growth. By His omniscience wisdom, God has inbuilt every ling creature with the ability of continuous growth and development. The beauty of that is to forestall monotony and makes living a continuously exciting adventure.

Thus, Adam and Eve would need to grow into their full inheritance of power and wisdom. While growing, God was keenly protecting them with His Fatherly regulations. Meanwhile, there in the Garden of Eden, the intruder, Satan, lurked sinisterly and patiently, waiting for the right time to strike with his evil plan.

Wasn't Adam, who was the head of the family, aware of a foreign intruder in his domain? Yes, he was aware, because nothing could enter the earth from another world without Adam's awareness. Adam and his wife, Eve, had been created and endowed with the ability to be in total control of the earth, and especially their home, the Garden of Eden.

Then how was it that Adam didn't challenge this foreign intruder, Satan, to ascertain the intruder's mission and take appropriate decision? How would a foreigner just enter his home without Adam reacting accordingly? The answers to these questions lie in the analysis of what happened to the Second and Last Adam, Jesus Christ (1Cor.15:45). Satan appeared to Jesus exactly the way he did to the first Adam. Here is the analysis of the encounter:

(1) Satan appeared in friendly pretence
Satan came pretending to be innocent, almost like a friend, to Jesus. The first words of Satan to Jesus vividly portrayed this. At the height of Jesus' hunger after a 40 days of praying and fasting, Satan appeared and whispered almost in a friendly manner: *"If you are the Son of God, tell these stones to become bread"* (Mat.4:3 NIV).

That was exactly what Satan did to the first Adam. He must have appeared quite innocently and friendly to Adam, making Adam not to suspect the evil intention of Satan.

(2) Satan's evilness was fully known
Interestingly, Jesus was fully aware of the cunning trick of Satan. He knew Satan was not and would never ever be a friend. He knew Satan, the Devil, was ultra-evil personified. He knew he was Lucifer before but his nature had been so disfigured that there was no iota of truth and goodness in him (Joh.8:44).

In the same manner, the first Adam must have known that Satan was despicable and malicious. How would he have known when he had never heard or seen Satan before? Don't forget Adam was a spirit being living in a physical body. Adam's eido centre of his spirit man would have picked the evilness of Satan just as Jesus' spirit man could pick information around Him during His earthly walk (Luk.9:47; Joh.2:23-25).

(3) Satan's scheme could be defeated with God's word
Knowing the despicable and malicious intention of Satan, Jesus countered the supposedly friendly words of Satan with the Word

of God: *"It is written: 'Man shall not live on bread alone, but on every word that comes from the mouth of God'"* (Mat.4:4 NIV).

In the same way, the first Adam could have countered Satan with the Word of God that designated his authority (Gen.1:28). Adam could have confronted Satan thus: "My Father has given me His lovely commandment for my benefit and you have no right to question such authority. Therefore, I command you to leave my home now." Sadly, Adam didn't counter Satan's intrusion; Adam's immaturity caused him the regrets and pains of his life. He allowed the intruder, Satan, to lurk around in his domain, thereby exposing his wife and his environment to the sinister danger posed by this evil trespasser.

The Subtle Attack

As he lurked sinisterly about,, Satan finally saw the opportune moment and that was when Eve was by herself. He sweet-tongued Eve:

> *"He (Satan) said to the woman, 'Did God really say, 'You must not eat from any tree in the garden'?" (Gen.3:1 NIV).*

Why did Satan target the woman and not the man first with his subtlety? Of course, Satan would have known that Eve was more gullible for manipulation with a sweet tongue than her husband was. But how did Satan know this when he had never seen a human female before? Obviously, Satan would have been watching and studying Adam and his wife, Eve, for some time, most likely from a distance on Earth or from Hell; in the spirit realm, distance is not a barrier at all.

Note how tactfully Satan warmed his way to Eve's mind and heart:

• Satan's aroused Eve's curiosity to attract her attention
He challenged Eve on what God had told them. When Adam was given the commandment not to eat from the fruits of the Tree of Knowledge of Good and Evil by God, Eve had not yet arrived on earth (Gen. chpt. 2). However, Adam had told her exactly what God commanded. Thus, Eve knew the commandment of God and attempted to correct Satan's defacement of God's instruction.

> *"The woman [Eve] said to the serpent, 'We may eat fruit from the trees in the garden, but God did say, 'You must not eat fruit from the tree that is in the middle of the garden, and you must not touch it, or you will die'" (Gen.3: 2, 3 NIV).*

By twisting the Word of God, Satan could get Eve's attention. Over these years, Satan used the same tactics. He looked for ways of getting one's attention.

Sadly, Eve didn't do what Jesus did by countering Satan with the Word of God given to her and her husband, Adam.

• Satan sweet-tongued Eve
Thus, when Satan saw that Eve's attention was aroused, he launched his next strategy, which was the sweet-talking. Satan sweet-tongued Eve by giving her a complete opposite information to God's instruction.

> *"'You will not certainly die,' the serpent said to the woman. 'For God knows that when you eat from it your eyes will be opened, and you will be like God, knowing good and evil'" (Gen.3:4,5 NIV).*

Whereas God clearly stated, "*when you eat from it you will certainly die" (Gen.2:17 NIV),* Satan countered with his words, "*You will not certainly die*" if you eat the fruit (Gen.3:4 NIV). In the end, Satan succeeded in deceiving Eve into eating the forbidden fruits of the Tree of the Knowledge of Good and Evil. Interestingly, Eve took the fruit to Adam, who also ate it.

Fig.14: Whereas God clearly stated, *"when you eat from it you will certainly die" (Gen.2:17 NIV)*, Satan countered with his words, *"You will not certainly die"* if you eat the fruit (Gen.3:4 NIV). In the end, Satan succeeded in deceiving Eve into eating the forbidden fruit of the Tree of the Knowledge of Good and Evil. Interestingly, Eve took the fruit to Adam, who also ate it.

Adam's Wilful Disobedience

But why would Adam eat the fruit knowing the full implication of such disobedience? Was he also deceived like his wife by Satan? Adam was not deceived.

"And Adam was not the one deceived; it was the woman who was deceived and became a sinner" (1 Tim.2:14 NIV).

If Adam was not deceived why did he receive the fruit from his wife? The Bible does not mention why Adam received the fruit from his wife. But it appears Adam did it as a result of:

- Love for his wife – Adam loved his wife right from the very day he sighted her. As a result of such love for his wife, Adam would have wanted to identify with her even in her failure.
- Fear of being left alone – Adam knew the consequences that would follow Eve's disobedience. He knew Eve would die. Most likely Adam would have been seeing animals die, and as such, must have known what it was to be dead. And considering what he suffered when he was alone, he wouldn't want to be in that shoe of loneliness again. He wouldn't want to be alone again when Eve died! He allowed fear to push him to do the unthinkable. He took the fruit from his wife and ate it, thereby identifying with his wife and damning the consequences of his action.

CHAPTER 20

THE JUDGMENT OF SATAN

THE DAY ADAM AND HIS wife ate the forbidden fruit of the Tree of the Knowledge of Good and Evil, God came down to the Garden of Eden as He used to do (Gen.3:8). However, this time, the relationship was no longer the same and the fellowship between the Father and His children was severed.

When they heard the sound of the Lord God walking in the garden in the cool of the day, Adam and his wife, Eve, hid themselves from the Presence of the Lord God among the trees of the garden. Then the Lord God called to Adam and said to him, *"Where are you?"*

Adam replied with a trembling voice, quite unlike his usually gracious audacity in the Presence of his Father: *"I heard Your voice in the Garden, and I was afraid because I was naked; and I hid myself."*

"Who told you that you were naked? Have you eaten from the tree of which I commanded you that you should not eat?" the Father enquired.

"The woman whom You gave to be with me, she gave me of the tree, and I ate," Adam mumbled in fearful tone as he shifted blame in an attempt to excuse his failure.

Then the Lord God said to the woman, "What is this you have done?"

The woman answered, "The Serpent deceived me, and I ate"
(Gen.3:8-13 NKJV).

WHAT A DAY!

What a day it was for this couple! What a mournful day; it's a day they wouldn't forget in a long time! A day of anguish and pains! A day of sorrow and sadness! A day the head of the family shifted blame and succumbed under the weight of mournful regret.

As the head of the family, it was in order that God had demanded of Adam to give account of his stewardship. What a lesson to us all, especially heads of families and those in leadership position of any establishment. Indeed, *"it is required in stewards that one be found faithful" (1Cor.4:2 NKJV).* Adam was not deceived like his wife; he simply failed the temptation of leadership!

Interestingly, immediately after eating the forbidden fruit, Eve knew that she had been deceived by the sweet-tongue of Satan, the Old Serpent. But it was too late. The deeds have been done. The harm has been wrought, and injustice has been perpetuated. Never again would they be the same perfect creatures that they were originally created. Never again would their progenies yet unborn become whom they were destined in God to be.

But didn't God see when they were being deceived and ate the forbidden fruit? Why didn't He stop them from eating the fruit?

Obviously, God, in His omnipresence, would have seen Adam and Eve eating the forbidden fruit. In addition, God is omnipotent, hence, He had the power to stop them from eating the fruit. But why didn't He stop them? The better question should be: Why did Adam and Eve cast off the restraining influence of the Holy Spirit of God and disobeyed God by eating the forbidden fruit?

Fig.15: When they heard the sound of the Lord God walking in the garden in the cool of the day, Adam and his wife, Eve, hid themselves from the Presence of the Lord God among the trees of the garden because of their disobedience. Then the Lord God called to Adam and said to him, *"Where are you?"* Adam replied with a trembling voice, quite unlike his usually gracious audacity in the Presence of his Father: *"I heard Your voice in the Garden, and I was afraid because I was naked; and I hid myself."* (Gen.3:8-10 NKJV).

Lack of Self-Control

God was not just the Creator but also the Father of Adam and Eve.

"...Adam – the son of God" (Luk.3:38 NKJV).

In other words, God was building a Family on Earth through Adam and Eve. As a Father, God, knowing the devastating impact of the lifestyle of Satan, not only gave His children, Adam and Eve, instructions on the need to avoid disobedience, but also provided the enabling power to counter disobedience. As children of God, Adam and Eve had the life (zoe) of God flowing through them. The Holy Spirit of God is the carrier of God's life. One of the functions of the Holy Spirit is restraining influence from sin. The Holy Spirit restrains God's children from sin. Such restraining power of the

Holy Spirit is imparted into the spirit man of an individual. It is also called 'self-control' in Galatians 5 verse 22.

Thus, the self-controlling or self-restraining power of God was in Adam and Eve, and this could have caused them to triumph over the deceptive attack of Satan. In other words, Adam and Eve had the power to conquer Satan but they disobeyed.

THE CONSEQUENCES OF DISOBEDIENCE

Disobedience to God's law means obedience to the opposition, which is Satan's. Adam and Eve cast off the restraining influence of the Spirit of God in their lives and hence sinned. That is, Adam and Eve disobeyed God and sinned. Sin has consequences, therefore, Adam and Eve had to face the consequences of their sins. Firstly, God pronounced judgment on Satan. Here are the divine judgments on Satan:

(a) Satan was debased below every creature

> *"Cursed are you above all livestock*
> *and all wild animals!*
> *You will crawl on your belly*
> *and you will eat dust*
> *all the days of your life" (Gen.3:14 KJV).*

God's judgment debased Satan the more. By that divine judgment, Satan was debased below any creature that ever lived. The once bright morning Lucifer was eternally condemned to Satan, and now further debased below all creatures.

(b) Dust became Satan's food

"And the Lord God said to the serpent, Because you have done this, you are cursed above all [domestic] animals and above every [wild] living thing of the field; upon your belly you shall go, and you shall eat dust [and what it contains] all the days of your life" (Gen.3:14 AMP).

Thus, part of Satan's debasement was that his food would be dust from henceforth, hence, anything that came from the dust became food for Satan. This includes the human body, which was formed from the dust. Sicknesses and diseases that ravage the body of man are all the after-effects of Satan's feeding on the human race.

(c) Enmity between Satan and the Seed of the Woman

"And I will put enmity between you and the woman, and between your offspring and her Offspring; He will bruise and tread your head underfoot, and you will lie in wait and bruise His heel"

(Gen.3:15 AMP).

Five Important Points

Divine judgment put a division between Satan and the Seed of the woman. Genesis chapter 3 verse 15 was a prophesy about a division that would occur between Satan and the woman's Seed. There are five points here, viz.

- Firstly, the term 'woman' refers to Eve, the wife of Adam
- Secondly, Eve the woman would produce a Seed. This Seed would crush Satan. Despite that, Satan would bruise the Seed's heel.
- Thirdly, from this Seed of the woman, offspring (children) would be raised. That is, the Seed of the woman would have offspring.
- Fourthly, Satan would also have offspring (children).

- Fifthly, there would be antagonism between the offspring (children) of the Seed of the woman and the offspring (children) of Satan.

The summary of these five points is that, with time, two species of mankind would arise – the offspring (children) of Satan and the offspring (children) of the Seed of the woman; these two would antagonise each other fiercely.

The Offspring of Satan

The intelligent questions are: (i) who is this Seed of the woman? (ii)where would Satan get his children from?

When Adam and Eve disobeyed God, they sinned. In other words, the life of Satan (sin) became transplanted into their nature. Thus, from thence they carried the same nature as Satan. That is, they became children of Satan and ceased to be children of God. Therefore, any offspring or children born through Adam and Eve would automatically inherit sin, the life of Satan. Hence, all children that would be born through Adam and Eve would be children of Satan carrying sin in their nature. Such offspring would never be children of God. This is how Satan would raise his offspring.

For this reason, Satan rejoiced exceedingly because he believed he had finally won the battle against God's purpose. All children that would be born by Adam and Eve would be his, and hence, he rejoiced because he would finally fill the earth with his offspring and perpetuate his original evil plan.

However, hearing of the offspring Seed of the woman, Satan would have thought God planned to create another man and woman through whom he would raise the Seed that will bear godly offspring. Hence, he must have geared up himself for the next challenge! But God is all-wise and all-powerful. The creature can never win a war against his Creator.

Chapter 21

The Judgment of the Woman

"Then God said to the woman, 'I will cause you to have much trouble [or increase your pain] when you are pregnant [in childbearing], and when you give birth to children, you will have great pain. You will greatly desire [the word implies a desire to control] your husband, but he will rule over you'" (Gen.3:16 EXB).

THE DISOBEDIENCE OF EVE BROUGHT three divine judgments on her and all female offspring of hers:

(1) Pregnancy complications

The woman, Eve, was created with the capacity to carry pregnancy, which was designed by the Creator to be the means of bringing humans to earth. The pregnancy process was originally designed to be pleasurable and problem-free. But following the disobedience of the woman, this was not to be. From henceforth, pregnancy would become an agonising process for the woman. Pregnancy would be complicated with troubles.

How is it that, despite little or no help, pregnancy morbidity and mortality among animals are almost zero while in humans they are a major problem? Infertility rate, preeclampsia and eclampsia, antepartum haemorrhage, miscarriages, and many other pregnancy complications are almost unknown among animals but not so with humans. This is the result of the fallout of the Fall of Man! Today, maternal mortality has been an index of defining healthcare development across the globe. A lot of complications are associated with pregnancies. Gynaecological and obstetric medical science have been trying to provide answers to these numerous pregnancy-associated problems without much success.

(2) Pain-Ridden Labour

In the same manner, labour, parturition, or childbirth (the process of birth delivery) would no longer be problem-free for the woman and her progeny but fraught with pains and complications. Thus, following the Fall in the Garden of Eden, labour has been associated with intense, almost unbearable degree of pains.

Animals deliver their babies almost free from any complications whereas the process of childbirth in human is filled with risks of all sorts. Abnormally prolonged labour, cephalopelvic disproportion, cord prolapse, stillbirth, and many other childbirth complications are common occurrences in humans but not in animals. This is due to the effect of the Fall of Man.

(3) Problem-ridden family

As stated severally, it was God who established the marriage institution by which the human family system would be realised. In the master plan of the Creator, the human family was to be the epitome of divine bliss and tranquillity on earth. However, the disobedience of the first human family changed all that. Since they now had sin (the life of Satan) instead of *zoe* (the life of God) running in their system and, thus, had ceased to be God's children, the harmony and bliss of family life henceforth became elusive.

The woman's nature would now want to rebel the man's leadership role and the man would want to lord and rule over the woman, hence, causing squabbles and discontent in the relationship. Therefore, 'katakata' would henceforth characterise the human home. Katakata is the Nigerian word for disharmony.

*"...thy **desire** shall be to thy husband, and he shall **rule** over thee"*
(Gen.3:16 KJV).

The original Hebrew word translated as 'desire' in Genesis chapter 3 verse 16 means 'having desire to control.' In other words, the woman would want to control the husband. Also, the Hebrew word 'rule' in that same passage means 'to lord or command,' which means the man would want to command or lord over the wife. Ruling is different from leading. Ruling means to lord over; the words of a ruler are final despite any other good opinion. On the other hand, to lead is to coordinate or to manage. An example of a ruler is a King while an example of a leader is a President.

The original divine plan was that a family would consist of the man as the head while the woman as the helper or companion with God as the Union Maker or the Foundation of the family. This divine plan was to engender harmony and smooth operation of the family unit. The man as the head was not to 'lord' or 'rule' over the wife but to lead the family unit into actualising the divine plan.

Adam was to be a leader over his family and Eve was to be his companion. But their disobedience caused reconfiguration of the human nature that rebelled against divine order. Consequently, instead of pure love from the man for his wife, lust and acrimony took over, and instead of companionship, fighting for lordship and control of the man by the woman became the new order. The original divine plan was reversed as a result of the Fall of Man. Instead of controlling their environments, humans would henceforth expend their energy fighting to control each other and Satan would have a field day feasting on them as 'dust.'

CHAPTER 22

THE JUDGMENT OF THE MAN

"Then to Adam He [God] said, 'Because you have heeded the voice of your wife, and have eaten from the tree of which I commanded you, saying, You shall not eat of it: Cursed is the ground for your sake; in toil you shall eat of it all the days of your life. Both thorns and thistles it shall bring forth for you, and you shall eat the herb of the field. In the sweat of your face you shall eat bread till you return to the ground, for out of it you were taken; for dust you are, and to dust you shall return'"

(Gen.3:17-19 NKJV).

The disobedience of the first human family brought divine judgment, and Adam, being the head of the family, came under three major curses:

(1) LOSS OF OWNERSHIP AUTHORITY OVER THE EARTH

The earth was made for humanity, and such authority was embodied in the first human, Adam.

"The heaven, even the heavens, are the Lord's; But the earth He has given to the children of men" (Psa.115:16 NKJV).

As Adam fell so was the loss of this authority over the earth. This was evident by the divine verdict pronounced on Adam (Gen.3:17,18).

The earth was created fruitful, productive, and fertile for human existence. There were no sufferings, pains, or sorrows. The earth was made for the sons of God. The authority of man on earth was the Dominion Mandate (see Page 120).

However, when Adam and Eve disobeyed God, the life of Satan (sin) became transplanted into their nature. Thus, from thence they carried the same nature as Satan. That is, they became children of Satan and ceased to be children of God. The zoe life of God in Adam and Eve ebbed out, and in its place was sin. That is, the nature of Adam and Eve was reconfigured to carry the sin-genome. The one to whom they had yielded therefore became their new master. Satan became the master of Adam and Eve, while they became slaves of Satan.

"Don't you know that you are slaves of anyone you obey?"
(Rom.6:16 CEV).

Any offspring or children born through Adam and Eve would automatically inherit the sin-genome, the life of Satan. Hence, all children that would be born through Adam and Eve would be children of Satan carrying sin in their nature. In other words, all of humanity came under Satanic bondage. Satan became the Master of humanity. That means, the Dominion Mandate was lost to Satan. In other words, the dominion of man over the earth was lost to Satan. Man was no longer the god of the earth; rather Satan became the god of the Earth.

"...the god of this world [Satan]..." (2Cor.4:4 CEV).

That is, Satan stole the dominion mandate of man. About 4000 years later, Satan bragged about this stolen mandate to Jesus, the Second Adam, in the Jordanian wilderness.

"Then the devil [Satan] led Jesus up to a high place and quickly showed him all the nations on earth. The devil said, 'I will give all this power and glory to you. It has been given to me, and I can give it to anyone I want to. Just worship me, and you can have it all'"

(Luk.4:5-7 CEV).

Satan boasted to Jesus that the earth has been given to him. Who gave it to him? Adam did. But Satan lied; Adam never willingly gave his Dominion Mandate to Satan; rather Satan stole it from Adam. Also, note that Jesus didn't refute the claim of Satan because Jesus knew about that transaction; rather Jesus was angry with the deceptive ownership of Satan over the earth, and as such, Jesus angrily rebuked Satan: *"Get thee behind me, Satan"* (Luk.4:8 KJV).

(2) SUFFERING BECAME HUMAN EXPERIENCE

"You will sweat and work hard for [By the sweat of your brow you will eat] your food" (Gen.3: 19 EXB).

The disobedience of Adam and Eve not only resulted in the loss of ownership authority over the earth, but it also brought suffering to humanity. Mankind would henceforth toil, labour, and grind themselves for their livelihood, a sharp contrast from the experience in the Garden of Eden. Poverty and hardship from thence became part of the human experience, quite contrary to the original plan of God.

Satan stole the Dominion Mandate of man and soon filled the earth with his lifestyle. No longer would the earth be the beautiful, fruitful, productive, and fertile home for human existence. From henceforth, the ground would yield thorns and thistles for man; the sons of men would sweat and toil for every profit they made. Therefore, poverty and hardship are effects of curses.

(3) DEATH BECAME HUMAN EXPERIENCE

By choosing to obey Satan rather than to obey God, the life of Satan (sin) became infused in the human nature while the life of God (zoe) that was in him ebbed away. Humans became children of Satan and slaves to sin. The final outcome of sin is death; this is the Law of Sin and Death, which states that *"the wages of sin is death"* (Rom.6:23 KJV).

> *"Do you not know that if you present yourselves as obedient slaves, you are slaves of the one you obey, either of sin resulting in death, or obedience resulting in righteousness?" (Rom.6:16 NET)*

Adam and Eve have presented or offered themselves as obedient slaves to sin, the life of Satan, the result was death. Thus, one of the consequences of the Fall was the introduction of death into the human experience. Man was created to live forever just like God. But sin introduced death into the human nature.

> *"Later you will return to the ground, because you were taken from it. You are dust, and when you die, you will return to the dust [to dust you will return]" (Gen.3: 19 EXB).*

Two Kinds of Death for Humans

Two kinds of death occurred once man became the child of Satan and yielded to sin:

(i) Spiritual Death
God had declared to Adam:

"And the Lord God commanded the man, saying, 'Of every tree of the garden you may freely eat; but of the tree of the knowledge of good and evil you shall not eat, for in the day that you eat of it you shall surely die'" (Gen.2:16,17 NKJV).

God had decreed that 'in the day' they disobeyed by eating the forbidden fruit, Adam and Eve would surely die. CEV rendered it very succinctly as follows:

"But the Lord told him, 'You may eat fruit from any tree in the garden, except the one that has the power to let you know the difference between right and wrong. If you eat any fruit from that tree, you will die before the day is over!'" (Gen.2:16,17 CEV).

That is, they would die that same day they ate the forbidden fruit. Indeed, Adam and Eve died 'in the same day' they ate the fruit. The first death they experienced was spiritual death. Spiritual death is the cessation, demise or loss of the life of God (zoe) in a being. In other words, a being is said to be spiritually dead when he becomes cut off from the life of God. Adam and his wife, Eve, lost *zoe* and were cut off from the life of God as a result of their disobedience. In place of zoe, they now had sin. In other words, they became spiritually dead the very moment zoe left their human nature. Hence, Adam and Eve became separated from God and died spiritually that same day.

All descendants of Adam and Eve would inherit the sin-genome. Because they carried sin, humans were doom to the flames of Hell, which is the eternal home of all beings that carry sin, the life of Satan, in their nature. Fallen humans were to end up in Hell with Satan and the demons. What a tragedy!

(ii) Physical Death

The second kind of death Adam and Eve experienced was physical death. Physical death is the cessation, demise or loss of the physical body. It is bodily or clinical death. The first human casualty of physical death was Abel, the second son of Adam and Eve. Abel was murdered by his jealous elder brother, Cain, the first human to be born (Gen.4:1-8).

Indeed, Adam and Eve's sin brought not just spiritual death but also physical death in the human experience. The Bible recorded that Adam lived for 930 years, and died thereafter (Gen.5:5). The Scriptures did not mention when Eve died physically, most likely she died shortly before or after her husband's death. The man with the longest lifespan in the history of humanity was Methuselah, the 8th generation from Adam. He lived and died at the age of 969 years (Gen.5:21-27; see SSB Book 4).

In other words, no human had ever lived upto a thousand years, which are actually equivalent to one day with God (2Pet.3:8). That is, no human had lived past 'a day,' hence, confirming what God had told Adam: *"If you eat any fruit from that tree, you will die before the day is over!"* (Gen.2:16,17 CEV).

In addition, the introduction of death in the human experience also meant the rise of sicknesses and diseases. God did not create sicknesses and diseases; rather, they were characteristics of sin, the life of Satan, just as poverty is also a characteristic of sin. As stated earlier, sin is the opposite of zoe. Just as the characteristic features of zoe include health, prosperity, light, etc. so also the characteristic features of sin include sicknesses, diseases, poverty, darkness, death, etc., which had become the experience of the fallen humanity.

CHAPTER 23

THE SEVEN STRATEGIES OF SATAN

MAN WAS CREATED WITH ENORMOUS power as a 'god' of his world. That is the Dominion Mandate. However, Satan could disarm man and his enormous power by clever tactics, which are worth a closer examination. The lessons from the Fall of Man are eternal warnings for us all. The tactics or strategies that Satan deployed to outwit Adam and Eve remain the same over these 6000 years of human history. These strategies are seven in number.

STRATEGY ONE:
SATAN SEEKS FOR THE AREA OF VULNERABILITY

Satan studied Adam and Eve from a distance to observe the area of their vulnerability. Satan studied and saw the innocence of Eve, and capitalised on her gullibility. Satan will always use your weak points to tempt you.

STRATEGY TWO:
SATAN ATTACKS DURING
MOMENTS OF TRANSITION

Adam and Eve were in their transition period into full maturity when Satan struck. That has always been Satan's strategy. Most stringent temptations that you encounter often occur when you are at the verge of breakthroughs or transiting from one phase of life to the next level. The transition period is often an emotion-filled moment, and Satan takes advantage of such a high emotional period.

STRATEGY THREE:
SATAN GETS ATTENTION BY A SWEET TONGUE

Satan is not stupid, but a spirit being full of subtlety.

"Now the serpent was more subtle than any beast of the field which Jehovah God had made" (Gen.3:1 ASV)

The term 'subtle' used to describe the serpent in Genesis chapter 3 verse 1 is from the Hebrew term *aruwm,* which is also translated as 'shrewd, crafty, sly, sensible, or prudent.' The Serpent refers to Satan (Rev.12:9; 20:2). He was once the beautiful Lucifer with great wisdom (see Chapter 6). But divine punishment changed him to Satan, who still deploys his shrewdness and subtlety to gain attention and win converts just as he did with some of the Morning Stars.

STRATEGY FOUR:
SATAN APPEALS TO SENSUAL PLEASURES

One subtlety of Satan is to evoke sensuality, thereby making the temptation appear pleasurable. Satan presented Eve with the desirability of the forbidden fruit, appealing to its sensual aspect. Many fall into sin because of the pleasure that it evokes. Sin is luring and appetising because of the pleasure in it.

However, Satan will never tell you that the pleasure of sin is generally short-lived and is soon overshadowed by sorrows and sadness. He always presents the good side to lure the simple-hearted to compromise their stand.

"the pleasures of sin [is] for a short time" (Heb.11:25 ISV)

Indeed, temptation will never present to you the negative consequences, but will always present the good side. Always, only the pleasure of indulgence is remembered at the height of temptation; many don't see the negative consequences of their decisions until after the pleasurable emotions of the temptation wane off.

STRATEGY FIVE:
SATAN OFTEN PRESENTS IN THE
COVER OF SECRECY

Satan is no longer Lucifer, the Shining One. Rather, he is now the Devil. One characteristic of this new nature is covertness or secrecy. He lives in secret and acts in secret. Darkness is a characteristic of secrecy. Satan's home, Hell, is impregnated with unimaginably thick darkness, reflecting his new nature of sin. Indeed, sin is always associated with some form of secrecy, darkness.

> *"Whoever is simple, let him turn in here;*
> *And as for him who lacks understanding, she says to him,*
> *Stolen water is sweet,*
> *And bread eaten in secret is pleasant.*
> *But he does not know that the dead are there,*
> *That her guests are in the depths of hell" (Pro.9:16-18 NKJV).*

Satan secretly came to Eve. He does this even today. Therefore, beware once a course of action has some covertness! Nevertheless, nothing remains covered forever.

> *"For nothing is secret that will not be revealed, nor anything*
> *hidden that will not be known and come to light" (Luk.8:17 NKJV).*

STRATEGY SIX:
SATAN TWISTS THE WORD OF GOD

Satan was once Lucifer the covering cherub, the guardian of sacredness of Divine Constitution. Thus, Satan fully knows about God's Laws, and he seeks to twist these laws to suit his evil motive. Satan will not give you the full truth in every situation.

This action of Satan is what some scholars refer to as *apostasy*. Apostasy simply means defacement, contradiction, or blasphemy of God's word. It is the twisting of God's Word to fit one's ideology. For instance, Satan's comments to Eve in Genesis chapter 3 verses 4 and 5 were an apostasy. He mixed God's words with his words, thereby distorting the truth. God never told Adam and Eve that they would not die if they ate the fruit of the Knowledge of Good and Evil. But Satan twisted the instruction to achieve his evil desire.

Satan has been using apostasy ever since. Apostasy is a lie, it is a deceit, and it is the language of Satan. It is the same language Satan used against Jesus during Jesus' earthly ministry (Luk.4:9-12); Satan quoted Psalms chapter 91 verses 11 and 12 out of context to Jesus, who countered the apostasy by using the Scriptures of Deuteronomy chapter 6 verse 16. That is, the knowledge of the Scriptures is the most effective weapon against apostasy.

STRATEGY SEVEN:
SATAN LUNGES DIRECT CONFRONTATION

When subtlety and deceit seemed to be failing, Satan then launched a direct assault against Eve. "Then the serpent said to the woman, 'You will not surely die'" (Gen.3:4 NKJV). This statement was an assault, a direct attack against Adam and Eve.

In other words, when compromise and deceit seem to fail, Satan often lunges a direct attack against children of God.

THE CDC DEVICES OF SATAN

In summary, the above seven strategies deployed by Satan can be summarised into three *CDC Devices,* also known as the *CDC Tactics*:

• **C = Compromise** – this is when Satan attempts to negotiate his way by intelligent argument. To achieve this, Satan first studies the vulnerability of his target and then approaches the target with sweet-tongue in order to cause the target to abandon his tough stand.

• **D = Deception** – this is when Satan twists the Word of God in order to deceive his target. Satan was once Lucifer the covering cherub in charge of divine laws, hence, he knows the Word of God. However, to achieve his evil purpose, he seeks to twist the Word of God. Therefore, Satan will only succeed if his victim does not have the full knowledge of the Word of God about the temptation.

• **C = Confrontation** – this is when Satan lunges a direct assault against his target. Satan often deploys confrontation when compromise and deception fail to achieve his purpose.

The CDC Tactics are the age-old devices of Satan. He deployed these three tactics when he was Lucifer to win about one-third of the Morning Stars over to himself in a battle he eventually lost (see Chapter 9).

In AD 30, Satan utilised the same tactics when he challenged Jesus, who is the second and last Adam, in the wilderness. Satan challenged Jesus with three temptations. The first temptation was when Satan asked Jesus to turn stones into bread. Jesus was in the conclusive phase of a forty-day praying and fasting, and was hungry at this stage. Satan saw it as a vulnerable moment to lunge an attack. Hence, he came to Jesus with sweet tongue, asking Jesus to compromise His position as the Son of God with the following words:

"If You are the Son of God, command that these stones become bread" (Mat.4:3 NKJV).

When his compromise tactic failed, Satan launched the next tactic, which was deception. He took Jesus to the top of the Temple and asked Jesus to jump down, quoting the Scriptures of Psalms 91 verses 11 and 12 to back up his words.

"If You are the Son of God, throw Yourself down. For it is written: 'He shall give His angels charge over you,' and, 'In their hands they shall bear you up, lest you dash your foot against a stone'" *(Mat.4:6 NKJV).*

Note that Satan deliberately twisted the Scriptures of Psalms 91 verses 11 and 12 to suit his evil intention. The Scriptures do not in any way enjoin anyone to jump stupidly and expect God's protection, rather the Scriptures state that in event of evil attack or danger, God will send his angel to protect and guide His people.

On seeing that his compromise and deception tactics did not succeed, Satan felt frustrated and decided to lunge an attack of direct confrontation. He took Jesus to a mountain where he showed Jesus all the vainglories and prosperity of earthly kingdoms, which he claimed ownership. Satan then confronted Jesus by demanding that Jesus should bow down and worship him so that he could make Jesus to be ruler over these dominions (Mat.4:8-10).

Note that for each of these three tactics (compromise, deception, and compromise), Jesus countered the Devil with the Word of God. Jesus used the weapon of the Word to overpower the evil devices of Satan. That is a lesson of all time for children of God. You can win all the devices of the Devil with the Word of God, which is a weapon.

In SSB Books 4 and 6, you will read about Church history on how Satan deployed these same tactics, the CDC Devices, to attack the early Church. Indeed, we are not ignorant of the devices of the Devil.

> *"lest Satan should take advantage of us; for we are not ignorant of his devices" (2Cor.2:11 NKJV).*

In the same vein, Satan and his demons will deploy the same tactics against you. They work through human agents to attack. It is the reason why diseases, sufferings, and anguish abound in the world. Like Jesus, your weapon of victory is the Word of God.

CHAPTER 24

THE INHERENT BENEFITS OF DEATH

ADAM AND EVE LOST THEIR home, the Garden of Eden, because of their disobedience. God banished them from Eden, and placed cherub angels to guard the entrance into Eden so as to prevent them from eating the fruits of the Tree of Life, which would have made them and their future offspring to live forever on earth in their fallen state (Gen.3:24). As children, we used to wonder why God wouldn't allow Adam and Eve to eat the fruits of the Tree of Life and live on forever on earth. Interestingly, the answer is not far-fetched.

Fig.16: Adam and Eve lost their beautiful home, the Garden of Eden, because of their disobedience. God banished them from Eden, and placed cherub angels to guard the entrance into Eden so as to prevent them from eating the fruits of the Tree of Life, which would have made them and their future offspring to live forever on earth in their fallen state.

PHYSICAL DEATH WIPES SINFUL LIMITATIONS

Once Adam and Eve failed, they ceased to be perfect creatures of God as sin corrupted their nature. All their offspring became sin-laden as the sin-genome was passed down from generation to another. Hence, the human spirit lacks the capacity to relate with God, the source of true success and all goodness. Rather, evil fills the heart of the fallen man. Wickedness, injustice, and diseases are all characteristics of the evil nature of the fallen man.

The spirit, soul and body of the fallen man lack the capacity to understand and process the God-standard of success for humanity. The scientific and technological advancement man had attained is an infinitesimal drop compared to the scientific and technological advancement in Heaven.

For instance, long before there were cars on earth, dwellers in Heaven had far superior modes of transportation. For example, in AD 35, after a successful witnessing to an Ethiopian eunuch in Gaza, Deacon Philip was 'caught away' to Azotus, which was a distance of about 60 kilometres (Act.8:26-40). That is, Philip was transported by the enablement of the Holy Spirit at a speed and a manner yet unrivalled in human scientific growth and development. In addition, after His resurrection, Jesus could bodily fly through the sky unhindered by gravitational forces and passed through a material wall bodily to meet with His frightened disciples. Prophet Elijah was transported to Paradise in a heavenly aircraft in about 850 BC, long before the Wright brothers, Orville and Wilbur, invented aeroplane in 1901 and the rocket propulsion device later.

These feats of transportation were but a negligible degree of advancement compared to the full weight of the glorious transport modalities in Heaven! Yet that was originally how God made man to function on earth as evidenced by the lifestyle of the last Adam, Jesus Christ. Sadly, the fallen nature of man wouldn't be able to understand such realities. The Fall brought gross limitation to the progress of man. Physical death is, therefore, a means of wiping off such limitations while waiting for the restoration of man's lost glory.

PHYSICAL DEATH – A MEANS OF RENEWING THE EARTH'S SURFACE

Physical death is a means of ridding off wickedness from the earth, and hence, renewing the earth's surface. That is, by preventing Adam and Eve from eating from the Tree of Life and, hence, stopping mankind living forever after the Fall on earth, physical death has inherent benefits to the fallen mankind. It is a divine wisdom to assist the fallen humanity so that no man would live forever in a sinful state. Physical death erases the evils of past people, thereby, renewing the surface of the earth.

THE LOVE OF GOD BEHIND THE COVER OF DEATH

Because eternity had been engraved in the human nature at creation, every person longs to live forever. No one wants to die. Eternity is in the heart of man; the genome of eternity was encoded in the heart of the human spirit at creation (Ecc.3:11). Death cuts short such an eternity prospect on the present earth, for all humans that come from fallen Adam and Eve inherit the sin genome of Satan and, hence, are natural products of death.

Living forever on earth with the sinful nature would have been the worst experience for man. God, in His omniscience, had foreseen such an awaiting disaster and crafted death as a means of avoidance of such disaster.

- Imagine if people like Adolph Hitler of Nazis Germany, Idi Amin of Uganda, King Herod of Jerusalem, Emperor Nero of Roman Empire, and many other wicked persons that walked in this world were still alive!
- Imagine living forever on earth with world infamous serial killers and rapists like Andrei Chikatilo, who was popularly known as 'The Butcher of Rostov,' 'The Red Ripper' or 'The Rostov Ripper,' convicted of the murder of 53 women and

children between 1978 and 1990, and was executed by gunshot in 1994 in former Soviet Union (BBC, 1999).
- Imagine if cerebral palsy babies are to live forever in that paralysed state; what a tragedy that would have been to their families!
- Imagine living forever in penury and ignorance, what untold suffering that would be on the individuals, families, and the world!

Hence, God has designed death as the solution to wipe off the sinful works of man from the earth while waiting for the full restoration agenda for humanity to kick-start. What an unfathomable love of the Father for man! It is the agape love of God towards man, whom He has created in His image and likeness!

CHAPTER 25

THE KINGDOM OF DARKNESS ON EARTH

THE FALL OF MAN IS not a theoretical or a mere theological expression. It is the reality of the human experience. It changed the destiny of humans from being children of God with *zoe* flowing through their nature to children of Satan with sin running through their new nature. Sin brought darkness, diseases, and death into the human experience.

THE KINGDOM OF DARKNESS

The Fall of Man means that Satan has stolen from man his home, Planet Earth and its galaxies. Hence, instead of Man, Satan became the god of this world (2Cor.4:4). Satan became the ruler of the world, having stolen the dominion authority of man. He wasted no time in establishing his stolen dominion authority in the world.

Having been with God and seen the systems of God's good governance while he was Lucifer the anointed covering cherub, Satan tried to reproduce the machinery of God's governance. He set up a hierarchical machinery of operation of darkness on earth, refers to as the ***Kingdom of Darkness*** by the Scriptures (Col.1:13; Rev.16:10).

The Kingdom of Darkness is operated by demons chosen by Satan, who is the overall ruler. Humans became their subjects, whom they could 'feed' upon as they so desire, after all the fallen humans are 'dust' to the Devil and his demons (Gen.3:14). The opposite of the Kingdom of Darkness is the Kingdom of God, also known as the Kingdom of Light or Kingdom of Beloved Son of God (Mat.6:33; Col.1:13). Any unregenerated human who is not born again in Christ Jesus carries a sin-genome in his nature, and such an individual belongs to the Kingdom of Darkness (see SSB Book 5 for more on this topic and on how to become a citizen of the Kingdom of God).

HIERARCHICAL STRUCTURE OF THE KINGDOM OF DARKNESS

However, Satan's attempts to set up a disciplined hierarchical structure of governance in his Kingdom of Darkness fails woefully as his structural arrangement has never been perfect; the forces operating Satanic government always antagonise each other and are often manipulating each other. That explains the reason why a spiritualist could use one demonic force to fight off the other.

The Bible identifies five main hierarchies that form the leadership structure of the Kingdom of Darkness (Rom.8:38,39; Eph.1:21; 6:12; Col.1:16). These five main hierarchical offices of Satan's Kingdom of Darkness are briefly described as follows:

(1) Ruler of Demons

This is the highest authority in the Kingdom of Darkness. ***Ruler of Demons*** refers to Satan (Mat.9:34 NKJV). Every other rank in Kingdom of Darkness is subordinate to the Ruler of Demons. That is, as Ruler of Demons, Satan controls all other demons and their human agents, hence, he is the king of the Kingdom of Darkness.

Satan is known as ***Beelzebul***, which means 'lord of the flies,' or 'lord of dung,' depicting his lordship control over his kingdom (Mat.12:24). Satan's lordship is completely evil with no iota of goodness at all, hence, he is also called the ***Evil One*** (Mat.13:19 KJV). Because of the vileness of his kingdom, Satan is also called ***Belial***, which means vileness (2Cor.6:15). He is called in Hebrews

Abaddon (Greek form is ***Apollyon***), which means a ***Destroyer*** (Rev.9:11), depicting the destructive nature of the Kingdom of Darkness.

> *"And they had as king over them the angel of the bottomless pit, whose name in Hebrew is Abaddon, but in Greek he has the name Apollyon" (Rev.9:11 NKJV).*

> *"The thief does not come except to steal, and to kill, and to destroy"*
> *(Joh.10:10 NKJV).*

Satan is the Thief, who stole man's Dominion Mandate and then unleashed destruction on humanity. In other words, Satan is not only the Ruler over demons, but he also controls fallen humanity, who has become 'dust' food for Satan (Gen.3:14). Therefore, after he stole man's Dominion Mandate, Satan became the ***Ruler of this World*** (Joh.14:30).

> *"I cannot speak with you much longer, because the ruler of this world is coming. But he has no power over me" (Joh.14:30 CEV).*

The above statement was made by Jesus during the last phase of His earthly Ministry in AD 33. Jesus calls Satan the 'Ruler of this World.' The term 'world' is from the Greek word *Kosmos*, which refers to humanity and its population groupings. Following the Fall of Man, Satan became the Ruler of Kosmos, ruling over all of humanity.

Satan moved "to and fro on the earth" (Job 1:7 NKJV), setting up systems of operation among humanity and demanding authoritarian worship, hence, he was also addressed as the ***'god of this Age'*** (2Cor.4:4 KJV). The term 'age' in 2Cor.4:4 is from the Greek word *aion*, which is also translated as 'world' and it refers to the systems of operation or established order of things. In other words, Satan as the Ruler of this World set up systems of operations among humanity immediately he stole Man's Dominion Mandate, and infiltrated the earth and its atmospheric region, hence, also refers to as the ***Prince or Ruler of the Power of the Air***.

"you once walked, following the course of this world [Greek: aion], following the prince of the power of the air, the spirit that is now at work in the sons of disobedience" (Eph.2:2 RSV).

Simply put, Satan holds the highest rank in the Kingdom of Darkness. He is the ***Old Serpent***, the ***Great Dragon***, the ***Devil***, the ***Deceiver of the Whole World*** (Rev.12:9). He deceived one-third of the Morning Stars to follow his rebellious treason (see Chapter 9), he deceived Eve that made Adam to fall, and he is presently deceiving humanity from following the Gospel of Christ, which is the only way for humans to become citizens of the Kingdom of God.

As stated on Page 104, the term 'devil' is from the Greek word *diabolos*, which means 'a being proned to slander or false accusation.' Satan always seeks to slander the way of righteousness and accuses those that have the zoe nature and are citizens of the Kingdom of God. Satan, which means an 'adversary,' stands in constant opposition against the Kingdom of God.

> *"Be sober, be vigilant; because your adversary the devil walks about like a roaring lion, seeking whom he may devour" (1Pet.5:8 NKJV).*

(2) Dominions

Dominions are what Ephesians chapter 6 verse 12 refers to as the ***Rulers of the Darkness*** of this world. They are territorial, that is, Satan put ruling demons in charge of territories in the world, e. g. the Prince of Persia that withstood and prevented answers to Daniel's prayers, and the Prince of Greece (Daniel chapter 10).

After Satan, who is the king of the Kingdom of Darkness, the next in command in authority are the Rulers of Darkness (or simply called ***Dominions*** in Eph.1:21 and Col.1:16 or ***Depths*** in Rom.8:38).

(3) Thrones

Thrones are referred to as **Spiritual Wickedness** in high places in Ephesians 6 verse 12 while Ephesians chapter 1 verse 21 refers to Satanic Thrones as **Might**. Romans 8 verse 38 refers to Satanic Thrones as **Height**.

It appears that these Spiritual Wickedness in high places are the ones that directly serve Satan and his interest in Hell. Individuals who have been to Hell often give tales of the unimaginable horrors and wickedness of the spiritual wickedness in high places.

Spiritual wickedness in high places keeps churning out wicked devices on earth through their human agents, especially at this end-time period of the world.

(4) Powers

Powers refer to commands or supremacies that are in charge of enforcing the wickedness of Satan in families and organisations. They are not territorial demons but can have influence over humans within the territorial sphere of a demonic Ruler of darkness.

In other words, **Powers** are demonic offices subordinate to the Rulers of Darkness. For example, the Prince of Persia apparently had other demonic agents that work directly under him, and these subordinates constituted the Powers of Persia.

(5) Principalities

Principalities are demonic forces that directly interfere in daily activities of man. They appear to be next in hierarchy to Powers. Principalities are the ones most individuals often confront in their daily activities, and they can oppress, possess, and cause obsession.

Examples of Principalities include the demonic legion that possessed the Gadarene man, whom Jesus set free in about AD 32 (Mar.5:1-20), the demonic spirit of divination that possessed the slave girl in Philippi that Apostle Paul cast out in AD 49 (Act.16:16-

18), and the evil spirits that disgraced the impostors, the seven sons of Sceva, in Ephesus in about AD 54 (Act.19:12-16).

Table 2: Hierarchical Ranks of the Kingdom of Darkness mentioned in Four Scriptures					
Scriptural Backup	**Principalities**	**Powers**	**Thrones**	**Dominions**	**Ruler of Demons**
Rom.8: 38, 39	Principalities	Powers	Height	Depth	Mentioned as part of Depth
Eph.1: 21	Principalities	Powers	Might	Dominions	Mentioned as part of Dominions
Eph.6: 11,12	Principalities	Powers	Spiritual Wickedness in high places	Rulers of the Darkness of this world	Mentioned as the Devil and as one of the Rulers of Darkness
Col.1: 16	Principalities	Powers	Thrones	Dominions	Mentioned as part of Dominions

Summary of the Chapter

The following points are the summary of the chapter:

- Satan with his principalities, powers, thrones, dominions, and fallen humanity constitute what the Bible refers to as the Kingdom of Darkness (Col.1:13; Rev.16:10). This kingdom is real and all humans of all generations born through Adam and Eve are citizens of this kingdom. The common characteristic feature of all citizens of this kingdom is that they all have the sin-genome, the life of Satan, in their nature.
- Immediately after the Fall of Man in the Garden of Eden, Satan systematically set up his Kingdom of Darkness over the entire earth. He set up systems to influence man's ideologies and activities. Soon the whole world came under

Satanic influence, and Satan boasted about this to Jesus in AD 30:

"Then the devil, taking Him up on a high mountain, showed Him all the kingdoms of the world in a moment of time. And the devil said to Him, 'All this authority I will give You, and their glory; for this has been delivered to me, and I give it to whomever I wish. Therefore, if You will worship before me, all will be Yours'" (Luk.4:5-7 NKJV).

Regarding the world, Satan boasted to Jesus " this has been delivered to me, and I give it to whomever I wish" (NKJV). That is, Jesus knew about the stolen Dominion Mandate of man by Satan from Adam, and He Jesus, the second and last Adam (1Cor.15:45), came to restore that lost mandate.

- The principalities, powers, thrones, and dominions are demonic installations with Satan as their leaders. These spiritual forces are real and they are not of the same influence. Each exercise influence according to the degree of the stolen authority Satan has allotted him. That explains why some spiritualists can use higher demonic influences to suppress other lesser ones.

- According to the *Law of Terrestrial Existence*, the only way these demonic forces can operate fully and unhindered in the materialistic world is to utilise human agents. That is, the Satan must obsess, oppress, or possess human bodies to be able to work their evil agenda on earth. Since humanity had lost authority over the earth, mankind became incapacitated in antagonising the evil machinations of these spiritual forces.

- The Kingdom of Darkness is real, and it rules on earth and in Hell, and its final destiny is in the Lake of Fire, where its rulers and citizens will be destroyed eternally. The opposite of the Kingdom of Darkness is the Kingdom of God, and fallen humanity can become citizens of the Kingdom through the Gospel of Christ (see SSB Book 5).

CHAPTER 26

AFTERMATHS OF SATANIC RULE ON EARTH: SUPERSTITION AND IDOLATRY

FOR 4000 YEARS FOLLOWING THE Fall of Man, Satan, using the stolen Dominion Mandate of Man, held sway with a supreme power of unleashing his lifestyle all over the surface of the earth. That is, from the time of Adam to about AD 30, which was when Jesus Christ started His earthly Ministry, Satanic Kingdom of Darkness reigned dominantly on earth among humanity.

According to Bible chronology, Adam arrived on earth in about 4176 BC, and he and his wife, Eve, fell to Satan's device shortly after Adam's arrival on earth (see SSB Book 4). The Scriptures did not state exactly how long Adam was on earth before the Fall, but it definitely occurred when he was less than 130 years old, which was the age of Adam when his third son, Seth, was born (Gen.5:1-3). In other words, the Fall of Man occurred few decades before 4046 BC, the year Seth was born.

Therefore, from about 4000 BC to about AD 30, Satan's Kingdom of Darkness ruled supreme among humans. An analysis of what took place in the world during those 4030 years graphically reveals the nature and lifestyle of the Kingdom of Darkness.

IGNORANCE AND SUPERSTITIONS

Man was a creature of power. Adam's intellect at creation was far beyond our present comprehension. He was the son of God and the 'god' of his world. Adam was the image and the likeness of His

Father. Ignorance was never a part of his nature. There was no challenge Adam wouldn't have a ready answer for. He was inbuilt with the capacity to be completely in charge of his home, Planet Earth.

Sadly, after the Fall, Adam's spirit man, which was the greatest asset of his life, died spiritually, and with such spiritual death came the loss of his capacity for outstanding ingenuity. Rather he became a victim of the elements of his world. He groped about in darkness, the very characteristics of his present sin nature.

Superstitions are products of ignorance. As a testimony of his new nature of sin inherited from Satan, superstition, with its twin sister idolatry, was the order of the day during the first 4000 years of human history. From Egyptian Empire to Assyrian Empire, Babylonian Empire, Persian Empire, Greek Empire, and Ancient Roman empire, superstitious beliefs held supreme on earth. From religion to commerce, from military activities to politics, et cetera, all were shrouded in superstitious mysticisms. The followings are some of the examples of superstitions and ignorance during the 4000 years of Satanic control of earth.

Military Superstitions in Egyptian, Assyrian and Babylonian Empires

The major wars that shaped the history of the world were all enmeshed with fetishism and superstitions. In 612 BC, in a bid to expand their territories, the Babylonians combined forces with the Medes, invaded and defeated Assyria, the then reigning power in Mesopotamia. That defeat drastically weakened Assyria. The Assyrians always prided themselves in their gods, whom they believed were represented by their kings. Therefore, Assyrian kings accorded themselves with titles such as *King of the Universe*, an audacious effrontery directed by Satan against God the Creator of the Universe, using the Assyrians as mere tools. As result of their theocratic power, the Assyrian kings were not only in charge of the armies but also every aspect of the Assyrian life.

Following the defeat of 612 BC, a lot of human sacrifices, libations, and many other ritualistic cleansing ceremonies were performed in Nineveh by the Assyrians to purge off the 'bad fate' they suffered in the hands of the Babylonians. Such superstitious beliefs were typical of the human race starting from the Fall of Man in the Garden of Eden.

Interestingly, while performing their religious ceremonies to curt the favour of their gods, the Assyrians also quietly contacted Egypt, the then dominant world power for assistance. Thus, three years after the defeat, the combined allied forces of Egypt and Assyria marched out against the rising neo-Babylonian Empire in about 609 BC at the Battle of Megiddo.

The Egyptian army was to pass through the outskirts of Judean territory on their way to Megiddo, but King Josiah of the Southern Kingdom of Judea (reigned: 640-608 BC) refused to give the Egyptians the right of passage. As a show of might, King Josiah rather marched his army against the forces of Egypt.

In the end, King Josiah was fatally wounded in the battle for which he eventually died and Pharaoh Necho II of Egypt annexed the Southern Kingdom of Judea. However, the Assyrian capital Nineveh and its town Harran were captured by the Babylonians, forcing the Assyrians to move their capital to Carchemish.

Again, the Assyrians took desperate measures of superstition, sacrificing their children to Assur, the Assyrian patron god while, at the same time, the Babylonian poured encomiums and libations to Marduk, the patron god of Babylon for their victory.

In 605 BC, four years after the Battle of Megiddo, the Egyptians and the Assyrians again joined forces against the combined armies of the Babylonians, Medes, Persians and Scythians at the Battle of Carchemish. Led by King Nebuchadnezzar II, the allied forces of Babylon destroyed the Assyrian and the Egyptian armies, thereby rewriting world history. Assyria ceased to exist as an independent power, and Egypt retreated and was no longer a significant force in the Ancient Near East, with the Babylonian Empire exerting unquestionable global authority.

These two battles (the Battle of Megiddo and the Battle Carchemish), like it was with other parts of the then world, were enmeshed with superstitious beliefs and ritualistic observations. Besides circular history like the Nebuchadnezzar Chronicles (also known as Jerusalem Chronicles), the two battles are recorded in the Bible: the Battle of Megiddo is documented in Second Kings chapter 23 verses 28 to 30 and Second Chronicles chapter 35 verses 20 to 27 while the Battle of Carchemish was detailed in the Book of Jeremiah chapter 46 verses 1 to 26. About seven centuries after King Josiah's death, Flavius Josephus, the first century Jewish historian, wrote a more detailed account of the battles in his work, Antiquities of the Jews, Book 10, chapter 5, section 1, apparently obtaining the extra account from other sources that are now lost.

Fig.17: A small kneeling bronze statuette believed to be Necho II, the Egyptian Pharaoh whose army fatally wounded King Josiah of the Southern Kingdom of Judea in the Battle of Megiddo in 609 BC. The statuette now resides in the Brooklyn Museum in the New York City, USA.

Military Superstitions in Persia and Greek Empires

Another decisive war that shaped the history of human civilisation was the Battle of Gaugamela in which Alexander the Great defeated Darius III of Persia in 331 BC. The war was a contest between the superiority of the Persian magic and Alexander's ingenuity and allegiance to the Greek gods. Both the Persians and the Greeks were all enmeshed with fetishism and superstitions.

Just before the combat, Alexander addressed his men, reassuring the typically superstitious Greek Macedonians that an earlier eclipse of the moon that appeared in the sky and an eagle that flew around their military camp were signs of victory (Wasson, 2012, Ancient History Encyclopedia: *Battle of Gaugamela*).

After the conquest, Alexander and his soldiers showered libations and countless sacrifices to the numerous Greek gods, whom they believed gave them the victory over Persia, and in essence, making Greece the new world superpower.

Military Superstitions in Roman Empire

Other major battles that shaped the history of the world were the three Punic Wars between the African Carthage and Rome (264-146 BC). These wars that decided the turn of events in human civilisation were all fraught with magic and superstitious rituals. For instance, at the height of despair, the Carthaginians threw some of their children into flames of fire to appease their god Moloch.

In another instance, in one of the defeats suffered by the Romans at the First Punic War, specifically at the Battle of Drepana (c.246 BC), the Roman Consul, Publius Claudius Pulcher, had to be withdrawn and sentenced to exile that ended his political career because he was convicted of committing sacrilege for impiously disregarded the divinations. According to writing of Marcus Tullius Cicero (106-43 BC), the sacred chickens had refused to eat, and Consul Claudius, in a fit of anger, threw the chickens into the sea: *"Since they do not wish to eat, let them drink!"* (Latin: "Bibant, quoniam esse nollent"), he was quoted to have said so (Cicero, 45 BC: *De Natura Deorum*, 2.7).

The superstitious Romans believed that their defeat by Carthaginians was due to Claudius' disregard of the sacredness of their gods when he threw the supposedly sacred chickens into the sea. The defeat at the Battle of Drepana and the committed sacrilege so demoralized the Romans that they waited seven years before building another fleet of ships to fight the Carthaginians.

These and many other battles fought in the first 4000 years of human history are good examples of how superstitions ruled the military and civilian lives of the nations of the world, a reflection of the despotic reign of the Kingdom of Darkness among humans.

Superstitions in Legal System

Legal systems of the first 4000 years of human history were collated codes of gross violations of the tenets of morality, and basic human rights were enshrouded in mystical superstitions. The celebrated Hammurabi Code, a compendium of 282 laws, created in ancient Mesopotamia in about 1754 BC contains many bizarre and gruesome forms of punishment and gross inequalities.

For instance, Hammurabi Code prescribed different punishments for men and women with regard to marital infidelity. Men were allowed to have extramarital relationships with maid-servants and slaves, but philandering women were to be bound and tossed into the great Euphrates River along with their lovers.

The Hammurabi Code contains violation of basic human rights as can be seen in some of its stipulations such as if a man killed a pregnant 'maid-servant,' the recommended punishment was only a monetary fine, but if he killed a 'free-born' pregnant woman, his own daughter would be killed as retribution.

The oldest known law code surviving today is the Code of Ur-Nammu, from Mesopotamia and is written on tablets, in the Sumerian language in about 2100–2050 BC. That is, the Code of Ur-Nammu is more than 300 years older than the Hammurabi

Code. The Code of Ur-Nammu, like the Hammurabi Code, sought to ensure morality and justice in the society, however, elements of superstition can be seen enshrined in its fabrics. For instance, one of its stipulations is that: *"If a man accused the wife of a man of adultery, and the river ordeal proved her innocent, then the man who had accused her must pay one-third of a mina of silver."* (Roth, 1995: *Law Collections from Mesopotamia and Asia Minor*, pages 13-22).

A river ordeal is a trial in which water is the testing agent to proof innocence or guilt. An accused person would be bound hand and foot and cast into a river or pond in which sinking or floating was taken as evidence respectively of innocence or guilt! What a superstitious belief!

RUDIMENTARY ARCHITECTURAL FEAT

The architectural success achieved by man within the first 4000 years of human history was also a far cry from today's reality. The architectural edifices were blanketed in mystical perception, which was a reflection of man's ignorance. For instance, all the seven wonders of the ancient world were a far cry of the present sophisticated architecture, and they were all shrouded in mysticism, being dedicated to demonic worship, as discussed below.

(i) The Great Pyramid of Giza

The Great Pyramid of Giza (constructed from about 2580 to 2560 BC) is the oldest of the Seven Wonders of the Ancient World, and the only one to remain largely intact. It was built as a tomb for the Fourth Dynasty Egyptian Pharaoh Khufu because of the deceptive knowledge about the afterlife, hence, it was also known as the Pyramid of Khufu or the Pyramid of Cheops. It was the tallest building in the world until the 14th century AD, when the Lincoln Cathedral was completed in England.

When it was completed by Khufu, the Great Pyramid of Giza was 481 feet (146 metre) in height, approximately the height of a modern 30-story office building. However, with the crumbling of some of the stones, the pyramid is slightly shorter today, measuring 455 feet (138 metres) in height.

Three smaller pyramids, often referred to as queens' pyramids, are located adjacent to Khufu's pyramid, and there is another smaller satellite pyramid that is located between the queens' pyramids and Khufu's. These queens' pyramids and the smaller satellite pyramid are believed to be built for members of Egypt's royal family.

Other notable pyramids of Giza are the Pyramids of Khafre and Menkaure, built by subsequent monarchs after Khufu. Close to the Pyramid of Khafre is the Great Sphinx of Giza, one of the oldest known monumental sculptures of ancient world, believed to have been built during the reign of the Pharaoh Khafre (c. 2558 – 2532 BC).

The Sphinx has the face of a human and the body of a lion. It is a large sculpture, measuring 240 feet (73 metres) long from paw to tail, 66.31 feet (20.21 metres) high from the base to the top of the head and 62 feet (19 metres) wide at its rear haunches. The face of the Sphinx is generally believed to represent the Pharaoh Khafre, indicating the superstitious belief of the monarch being elevated to the status of a god.

Each pyramid and the Sphinx had a mortuary and a valley temple, with a causeway connecting them. Seven boat pits were found at Khufu's pyramid, two on the south side, two on the east side, two in between the queens' pyramids and one located beside the mortuary temple and causeway. The best preserved boat, carefully reassembled from more than 1200 pieces, is 142 feet (43 m) long, with wooden planks and oars. The purpose of these boats is the superstitious belief in the afterlife – the boat were to help the dead to successfully transport to the ancestral world.

The Great Pyramids and the Sphinx, built on Giza Plateau, held spiritual significance to Egypt and the rest of the world for over 2000 years, as their images appeared in Levant, Persia, India,

Indonesia and elsewhere. It was used intensively as some sort of demonic cult initiation centre with a number of cults even today linking their roots to the Great Pyramid.

Interestingly, in late AD 2010, about 400 malnourished people, buried with few grave goods, carbon-dated to about 2000 years ago, were found in Giza, near the Great Pyramid. Apparently, the burial near the Great Pyramid was due to the superstitious belief that the dead will be transported to their ancestral home with the plateau of Giza, an Egyptian city on the west bank of River Nile, near Cairo, being the shortest and surest departure zone to the great beyond.

Fig.18: The Sphinx and the Great Pyramids of Giza.
The Great Pyramids and the Sphinx held spiritual significance to Egypt and the rest of the world for over 2000 years, as their images appeared in Levant, Persia, India, Indonesia and elsewhere. It was used intensively as some sort of demonic cult initiation centre with a number of cults even today linking their roots to the Great Pyramid.

(ii) The Temple of Artemis

Before the 7th century BC, the Carians and the Lelegians inhabited the ancient city of Ephesus. They constructed a temple devoted to the idol Cybele, goddess of abundance, whom they called the 'Great Mother.' The Ionians later infiltrated Ephesus, and renamed the goddess Cybele as Artemis. They built a temple with a wooden statue devoted to Artemis. But the wooden temple was destroyed by a flood in the 7th century BC. The Lydian king, Croesus, who invaded Ephesus at that time, decided to rebuild the destroyed temple with stones and adorned it with columns. This was the Temple of Artemis.

Fig.19: The Temple of Artemis in Ephesus.
This model of the Temple of Artemis is at Miniatürk Park,
Istanbul, Turkey, in an attempt to recreate the appearance of
the destroyed temple.

The Temple of Artemis, a Greek temple dedicated to the goddess Artemis, located in Ephesus (near the modern town of Selçuk in present-day Turkey), was one of the seven wonders of the ancient world. In 356 BC, a man named Herostratus, who had been in search of fame, succeeded in burning down the Temple of Artemis. The incidence was said to have taken place on the very night Alexander the Great was born. For this reason, Ephesians believed that Artemis did not save her temple because she was busy far away, attending to the birth of Alexander. This was one of the superstitions that fuelled the divinity of Alexander the Great even while he was a child. The Ephesians later reconstructed the temple of Artemis, adorning it with artistic beauty.

When Alexander the Great visited Ephesus in 334 BC, after defeated the Persians, he was greatly impressed by the Temple of Artemis, and he organized a military parade in order to pay honours to the goddess Artemis. Alexandra also promised the Ephesians to reconstruct the temple to adorn it with more beauty. However, the Ephesians refused that offer, telling Alexander that it was not fair for a god (referring to Alexander) to build a temple for another god (referring to Artemis).

Fig.20: Artemis (Diana), addressed as the 'Great Mother' and was worshipped as the goddess of abundance, an example of idolatry that Satan had perpetrated across the world in an effort to exert his Kingdom of Darkness among humanity.

During the era of the Roman Empire, the Romans named the goddess Artemis as Diana, hence, the Temple of Artemis was also known as the Temple of Diana. The temple held one of the dire religious fanaticisms in the ancient world as it kept churning out superstitious proclamations that spellbound the world until the advent of Christianity destroyed such Satanic stronghold on humanity.

In AD 55, Demetrius and his colleagues instigated a riot, claiming Apostle Paul and the young Church in Ephesus were disloyal to the Temple of Artemis and had won converts from its superstitious worship (Act.19:21-41). About 42 years later (AD 97), Timothy, Paul's co-worker and the Bishop of Ephesus, halted the festival of Katagogia, a demonic procession in honour of the goddess Diana (Artemis) and its Temple. That infuriated the superstitious pagans, who stoned the 80-year old Bishop Timothy to death (see SSB Book 6).

Notwithstanding, the seed of the Kingdom of God had been sown, and like a mustard seed, it grew to overshadow the demonic practices of the Kingdom of Darkness that were carried out in the Temple of Artemis so much that the temple worship was largely abandoned by late third century because of massive conversions to Christianity, and by AD 401, the temple was destroyed, and some of its stones were used to erect the columns of Hagia Sophia, a large Church cathedral in Constantinople (present Turkey).

(iii) The Hanging Gardens of Babylon

Another testimony of the impact of the Kingdom of Darkness on humanity was the mystical Hanging Gardens of Babylon, built in the ancient city of Babylon, near present-day Hillah in the Babil province of Iraq, by the Neo-Babylonian king Nebuchadnezzar II, who ruled between 605 and 562 BC.

King Nebuchadnezzar built the gardens for his wife, Queen Amytis. She was from Media, which was in present-day north-west Iran and south-east Turkey. In the hot and dry climate of Babylon,

Queen Amytis missed the trees, plants and mountains of her homeland, hence, Nebuchadnezzar built the Hanging Gardens to mimic her homeland and make her less homesick.

Though supposed to serve as a recreational centre for the king and his nobles, the Hanging Gardens were turned into centres for idolatry. The Tower of Babel, where God gave different languages to mankind to confuse the builders of the tower from carrying on with their disobedient act (Gen.11:1-9; see SSB Book 4), was said to be located close to the Hanging Gardens.

Fig.21: A 3-D reconstruction of the Hanging Gardens of Babylon (by Elena Terletska/Fotolia)

(iv) The Colossus of Rhodes

Similarly, the Colossus of Rhodes, the tallest statue of the ancient world, about 110 feet (33.53 metres) tall atop a 49-foot (14.9 metres) platform, constructed from 292 to 280 BC in the Greek city of Rhodes, was a statue devoted to the superstitious cult worship of the Greek titan-god of the Sun, Helios.

One of the Seven Wonders of the Ancient World, the Colossus of Rhodes was constructed by Chares of Lindos, a Greek sculptor, to celebrate the victory of the City of Rhodes over Antigonus I Monophthalmus, the ruler of Cyprus, whose son Demetrius I of Macedon unsuccessfully besieged Rhodes in 305 BC. The dedication script of the Colossus of Rhodes, preserved in Greek anthologies, shows the superstition attached to this statue:

> *"To you, O Sun, the people of Dorian Rhodes set up this bronze statue reaching to Olympus, when they had pacified the waves of war and crowned their city with the spoils taken from the enemy. Not only over the seas but also on land did they kindle the lovely torch of freedom and independence. For to the descendants of Herakles belongs dominion over sea and land."*
>
> *(Meleager of Gadara, c.60 BC: Anthologia Graeca, vol.4, p.171).*

The Colossus of Rhodes stood for 54 years until Rhodes was hit by an earthquake in 226 BC that resulted in significant damage to large portions of the City of Rhodes. The statue was broken at the knees and fell over onto the land. Ptolemy III Euergetes (284-222 BC), the then king of the Ptolemaic dynasty of Egypt, offered to pay for the reconstruction of the broken statue. However, the Pythia (the high priestess of the Temple of Apollo at Delphi) made it clear that the Oracle of Delphi objected to the reconstruction. The fear of offending the demonic gods Apollo and Hellios, therefore, prevented any reconstruction work on the statue.

According to Strabo (c.64 BC – c. AD 24), a Greek philosopher and historian, the remains of the statue of the Colossus of Rhodes laid on the ground for over 800 years, becoming a tourist attraction (Strabo, AD 23: *Geographica*, XIV. 2.5).

When the Arab military force captured Rhodes, the bronze statue of the Colossus of Rhodes was sold to a Jewish merchant of Edessa, who broke the statue into smaller pieces and carted them away on 900 camels in AD 653.

Fig.22: The Colossus of Rhodes, the tallest statue of the ancient world and one of the then seven wonders, constructed in 280 BC, was dedicated to Helios, the Greek Sun god, another testimony of the rule of the Kingdom of Darkness amongst humanity.

(v) The Statue of Zeus

Paganism is shrouded in superstition and it wholly ruled the thoughts, words, and actions of men during the first 4000 years of human history. Paganism was one method Satan used to perpetuate his rule amongst humanity.

The Statue of Zeus at Olympia, a giant seated figure, about 13 metres (43 feet) tall, made by the Greek sculptor Phidias around 435 BC at the sanctuary of Olympia, Greece, is a clear example of how Satan filled the thoughts, words and actions of men using paganism.

In about 440 BC, the renowned Greek sculptor Phidias made a massive statue of the goddess Athena Parthenos and housed the statue in a temple called Parthenon that was built at the Acropolis (a citadel) of Athen. Seeking to outdo their Athenian rivals, rulers of Eleia, an ancient district in present-day Elis region of Western Greece and custodians of the Olympic Games, in about 435 BC, commissioned Phidias to produce a sculpture of Zeus for their recently constructed Temple of Zeus. The statue was finished and dedicated in about 430 BC.

The Statue of Zeus, one of the seven wonders of the ancient world, was another evidence of superstition and idolatry that perverted the earth. A notable instance was recorded by Livius Titus (59 BC – AD 17), a Roman historian, popularly known as Livy. According to Livy, the military general Aemilius Paulus (c. 229 – 160 BC), a Roman consul, conquered Macedon during the Third Macedonian War (171–168 BC). Paulus then toured the conquered territories, among which was Eleia, where he visited Olympia town. According to Livy, when Paulus saw the Statue of Zeus at Olympia, he was "moved in the depth of his soul" as if he had "gazed on...the very person of Jupiter," the Roman equivalence of Zeus, and he, as such, ordered a lavished sacrifice to Zeus.

> *"Then he [Paulus] visited Sparta, a place memorable not for the magnificence of its public buildings but for its discipline and its institutions; from there he went up to Olympia by way of Megalopolis. At Olympia he saw many sights which he regarded as well worth a visit; but he was moved in the depth of his soul when he gazed on what seemed like the very person of Jupiter. For that reason he ordered a sacrifice to be provided on a more lavish scale than usual, just as if he had been going to offer sacrifice on the Capitol." (Livius Titus, 9 BC: Ab Urbe Condita, XLV. 28, 5).*

In another instance, the first century AD Greek orator Dio Chrysostom declared superstitiously that a single glimpse of the statue would make a man forget all his earthly troubles.

> *"For verily even the irrational brute creation would be so struck with awe if they could catch merely a glimpse of yonder statue, not only the bulls which are being continually led to the altar, so that they would willingly submit themselves to the priests who perform the rites of sacrifice, if so they would be giving some pleasure to the god, but eagles too, and horses and lions, so that they would subdue their untamed and savage spirits and preserve perfect quiet, delighted by the vision; and of men, whoever is sore distressed in soul, having in the course of his life drained the cup of many misfortunes and griefs, nor ever winning sweet sleep — even this man, methinks, if he stood before this image, would forget all the terrors and hardships that fall to our human lot."*
> *(Dio Chrysostom, AD 97: Discourses, 12.51).*

Sadly, history has shown that the idolatry worship of Zeus only bred inhumane injustices, which were what the ruler of darkness, Satan, had desired, for he was a murderer and a pervert of justice. Indeed, covert human sacrifices were common practices connected with the Temple of Zeus and denial of human dignity with gross abuse of human rights of non-citizens was perpetuated by the worship of Zeus. Licentiousness with sexual promiscuity was a common practice with the worship of Zeus. The Statue of Zeus and its temple became the most revered and feared of all deities during this period of ignorance when the Kingdom of Darkness reigned unchallenged among mankind.

However, as the light of the glorious Gospel spread within the Roman Empire and around the world, people began to see the deception and retrogression associated with idol worship. In AD 391, the Roman Emperor Theodosius I, who was disgusted with the superstition of idolatry and became converted to Christianity, banned participation in pagan cults and closed the idol temples. Thus, the Temple of Zeus at Olympia fell into disuse.

Four years after the official banning of pagan worship (AD 395) by Emperor Theodosius I, the statue of Zeus was removed to Constantinople, the then capital of the Eastern Roman Empire, and kept in the Palace of a eunuch, Lausus, who was noted for acquiring a large collection of antiquated arts and sculptures. The statue was finally destroyed by a fire that razed down the Palace of Lausus in AD 475.

Another historical version claimed that the Statue of Zeus was destroyed by earthquakes just as its temple, Parthenon, at Olympia was destroyed by earthquakes in AD 522 and AD 551 after it was desecrated and abandoned in AD 426 following a decree against pagan temples by another Christian ruler, Emperor Theodosius II.

Fig.23: The Statue of Zeus at Olympia.
Zeus was the patron Greek god of the sky and thunder who lived on Mount Olympus. Its worship was filled with human sacrifice, licentiousness and sexual promiscuity, a clear tale of the perverted Kingdom of Darkness among humanity in the first 4000 years of man's history.

(vi) The Mausoleum of Halicarnassus

Even the Mausoleum of Halicarnassus or Tomb of Mausolus, a tomb built between 353 and 350 BC at Halicarnassus (present-day Bodrum in Turkey), is also an example of the ancient world paganism with its superstitious beliefs.

Mausolus was a regional governor (satrap) of the Persian Empire, and he married his sister, Artemisia II of Caria. When Mausolus died, his wife, Artemisia hired two architects, Satyros and Pythius of Priene, to design a grandiose tomb. Once the design was done, Artemisia then employed four famous sculptors to make sculptures for the four sides and the roof of the tomb. Each sculptor worked on one side of the tomb, embellishing it with scenes of Greek mythology, sculpted images of lions, horse-driven war chariots, and sculptures of many different gods and goddesses, with the pyramid-shaped roof crowned with a massive sculpture of a chariot in which Mausolus and Artemisia rode. This tomb of Mausolus, measuring approximately 45 metres (148 feet) in height, was called Mausoleum, which became the generic term for a monumental tomb.

As a testimony of the darkness that filled the earth orchestrated by the unchallenged rule of Satan over the first 4000 years of human history, the Mausoleum, also one of the seven wonders of the ancient world, was turned into a monumental shrine for cultism and ancestral worship. It partly survived successive earthquakes from the 12th to the 15th century, until it was completely dismantled in AD 1404 when the Knights of Saint John arrived at Halicarnassus and in AD 1494 carted away the broken pieces of the Mausoleum marbles to build the Bodrum Castle of Saint Peter.

Fig.24: The Mausoleum of Halicarnassus.
As an evidence of the darkness that filled the earth orchestrated by the unchallenged rule of Satan over the first 4000 years of human history, the Mausoleum, also one of the seven wonders of the ancient world, was turned into a monumental shrine for cultism and ancestral worship.

(vii) The Lighthouse of Alexandria

Navigation and space exploration during these 4000 years were regrettable as only paltry success was made. Instead of astronomy, it was astrology, and instead of heliocentralism it was geocentralism. People at one corner of the earth wouldn't dare to venture all out to other corners because of barbarism and the fear of falling into another planet on reaching the 'flat edge of the earth.'

The marginal achievement in navigation was the Lighthouse of Alexandria (also called the Pharos of Alexandria), constructed for about twenty years starting in 290 BC by Ptolemy II Philadelphus, the ruler of Egypt (280-247 BC), who decided to build the Lighthouse to guide sailors into the port. The Lighthouse was the third longest survivor of the seven wonders of the ancient world (the other two being the Mausoleum of Halicarnassus and the Great Pyramid of Giza).

The fullest description of the Lighthouse comes from Arab traveller Abou Haggag Youssef Ibn Mohammed el-Balawi el-Andaloussi, who visited Alexandria in AD 1166. According to the description, the Lighthouse was constructed from large blocks of light-coloured stone as a tower that consisted of three tapering tiers – a lower square section with a central core, a middle octagonal section, and, at the top, a circular section. At its apex was positioned a mirror which reflected sunlight during the day and a fire would be lit at night. It had an estimated height of 330 feet (100 metres), making it one of the tallest buildings of ancient world.

Extant Roman coins struck by the Alexandrian mint show that a statue of Triton, a Greek god believed to be the messenger of the sea, was positioned on each of the building's four corners while a statue of Poseidon, the Greek god of the sea and father of Triton, stood atop the lighthouse. The Pharos's masonry blocks were interlocked, sealed together using molten lead, to withstand the pounding of the waves. Facing the eastern side of the sea was an inscription on the Lighthouse that was dedicated to Zeus, the Greek god of the sky and thunder.

The Lighthouse survived three earthquakes between AD 956 and 1323, when it then became an abandoned ruin, until AD 1480, when the last of its remnant stones were used to build the Citadel of Qaitbay, defensive fortress built close to the site of the Lighthouse. In 1994, some French archaeologists discovered remains of the lighthouse on the floor of Alexandria's Eastern Harbour, and presently the government of Egypt is planning to build an underwater museum, using the ruins of ancient Alexandria, including those of the Lighthouse.

Fig.25: The Lighthouse – the third longest survivor of the seven wonders of the ancient world.
A statue of Triton, a Greek god believed to be the messenger of the sea, was positioned on each of the building's four corners while a statue of Poseidon, the Greek god of the sea and father of Triton, stood atop the lighthouse. Facing the eastern side of the sea was an inscription on the Lighthouse that was dedicated to Zeus, the Greek god of the sky and thunder.
Satan Has Nothing Good to Offer

Indeed, the Great Pyramid of Giza, Colossus of Rhodes, the Temple of Artemis, the Hanging Gardens of Babylon, the Statue of Zeus, the Mausoleum of Halicarnassus, and the Lighthouse of Alexandria were regarded as the seven wonders of the ancient world; that is, they were the best the ancient world could deliver despite such a protracted period of existence of about 4000 years, which was the period the Kingdom of Darkness held sway on earth without any challenge.

All the major successes made thus far in medicine, telecommunication, technology, construction, agriculture, commerce, legal system, et cetera, only came after the Kingdom of God was established on earth and started to dispel off the Kingdom of Darkness. In other words, Satan has nothing good to offer anyone, and this should be a warning for all time.

CHAPTER 27

AFTERMATHS OF SATANIC RULE ON EARTH: POVERTY AND DISEASES

SATAN INFILTRATED THE EARTH, FILLING the hearts and minds of men with darkness, with no measurable success to show for except superstitious beliefs. Every single decision was shrouded in superstition. It was no wonder for a good 4000 years, humans witnessed only shabby success. Indeed, *"sin is a reproach to any people"* (Prov.14: 34 KJV).

A review of achievements made by man within the first 4000 years of human history shows paltry rudimentary inventions in communication, agriculture, and architecture. Satan's rule generated darkness of ignorance and superstitions with virtually little attainments in human history.

The best form of communication invented was ancient hieroglyphic writing, which was invented in Egypt in about 2800 BC. In agriculture, irrigation systems and horticulture were practised along coastal regions such as at the borders of Nile River, but still they were subsistent and nomadic, a far cry from modern sophisticated agricultural practices.

POVERTY – THE IDENTITY OF THE KINGDOM OF DARKNESS

Adam was made and placed in the Garden of Eden, a place of great splendour and riches. Poverty was never part of his existence. He came in contact with poverty immediately after the Fall. Sin, the life of Satan, produced poverty in Adam. Famine, unfruitful toiling, and frustrations became part of the human experience following the Fall.

Mammon, the demon in charge of money, took over, producing the love of money in the hearts of humans, making people to love money than loving their Creator and their fellow humans. Those who had access to wealth enriched themselves greatly at the expense of the less privileged. Feudalism, totalitarianism, and other forms of political hegemony perpetuated poverty.

Inequality was gross and perpetuating as the first 4000 years of human history was enmeshed in survival of the fittest. Love, morality, and purity that characterised the human spirit were replaced with wickedness, lewdness and impurity of all shades and degrees. Indeed, the first 4000 years of human arrival on earth were a despicable epoch in the history of mankind, a testimony of the decadence orchestrated by the Kingdom of Darkness. Poverty is the identity of the Kingdom of Darkness!

DISEASES – SATAN'S LIFESTYLE

Diseases and sicknesses ravaged the human body with little or no resistance to counter them during the first 4000 years of human existence. Healthcare was shrouded in superstitious beliefs as ignorance reigned supreme. Medical and nursing practices were a far cry from what we have today. Weeping, sorrow, and pains ravaged the bodies of human. Indeed, the first 4000 years of human existence was the reign of Satan on Earth.

The origin of medical practice, like most other fields, is attributed to Africa, in the Ancient Egypt. Imhotep (c. 2650–2600 B), who served under the Third Dynasty of King Djoser as chancellor to the Pharaoh and high priest of the sun god Ra at Heliopolis, is credited with being the founder of ancient Egyptian medicine. He is also credited with being the original author of the Edwin Smith Papyrus, which detailed cures, ailments and anatomical observations. The

Edwin Smith Papyrus is regarded as a copy of several earlier works and was written about 1600 BC. It is an ancient textbook on surgery enmeshed in some magical thinking.

Along with the Egyptians, the Babylonians introduced crude practices of diagnosis, prognosis, physical examination, and remedies, all intertwined with magical prowess. The most extensive Babylonian medical text is the Diagnostic Handbook written by the ummânū, or chief scholar, Esagil-kin-apli of Borsippa, during the reign of the Babylonian king Adad-apla – iddina (1069-1046 BC). The Diagnostic Handbook introduced crude methods of therapy and aetiology with gross superstitious recognition.

During these periods, various other cultures in the Middle East, Africa, India, and China were noted to have developed crude forms of medical practices that were all shrouded in mysticism and superstition.

Hippocrates (c.460-c.375 BC) and his Coyan School produced the famous physician oath, the Hippocratic Oath. This has been translated into modern terms for today's medical practice, and all physicians around the world, on graduating from medical schools, often swear allegiance to the oath before they are registered to practice medicine. The original version of the Hippocratic Oath unveils the superstitions:

> *"I swear by Apollo the physician, and Aesculapius the surgeon, likewise Hygeia and Panacea, and call all the gods and goddesses to witness, that I will observe and keep this underwritten oath, to the utmost of my power and judgment..."*
>
> *(Hippocrates of Kos, c.400 BC).*

The last statement in the Hippocratic Oath is:

> *"If I faithfully observe this oath, may I thrive and prosper in my fortune and profession, and live in the estimation of posterity; or on breach thereof, may the reverse be my fate!"*
>
> *(Hippocrates of Kos, c.400 BC).*

Hippocrates and his students believed that Fortune was the blessing of the goddess Fortuna, the Latin version of the Greek goddess Tyche, renowned as the goddess of fortune and personification of luck. She might bring good or bad luck. Again, this attests to the shallow degree of human development and ignorance that enveloped the entire world as Satan reigned supreme for the first 4000 years of human existence, causing humans to ascribe all glory, worship and adoration to him rather than the true God, the Creator of the universe and the Author of all good things!

CHAPTER 28

TODAY'S EVIDENCES OF EXISTENCE OF SATAN AND DEMONS

ALL OF US OFTEN COME in contact with the reality of spiritual existence. From time to time, we come into contact with forces that baffle our natural explanation. We may tend to explain away such experiences with modern terminologies, the reality is that Satan and demons exist. If there is a Jesus Christ, then there is no doubt Satan and demons do exist because Jesus discussed Satan a lot in His messages.

In the medical and nursing fields, we come into contact with a lot of demonic activities. This chapter discusses some of the numerous cases I have witnessed in my medical practice.

JANE AND HER TALE OF MISFORTUNES

Jane was a regular patient at our clinic. She had graduated from the University of South Africa with a diploma in accountancy, and secured a job in a good firm. According to her, in January 2017, she experienced the New Birth and became regenerated (born again) in Christ. Immediately that happened, it seemed all hells were let loose. Things that were hitherto working well suddenly became complicated.

"Instead of life becoming easier, things became more and more tough and difficult," she cried. Her boss, who was in good terms with her, suddenly became difficult and unapproachable to her. She was still doing her job faithfully as usual, yet she seemed to

be running into troubles at work incessantly. She tried harder and harder to do her job, but no one seemed to notice how hard she worked. Tension mounted as she sensed she might soon lose her job and her financial security.

More so, the fortunes of the small business she ran from home suddenly started dwindling. The once profitable endeavour nosedived as her customer base shrank and her income gradually diminished. She opened up to discuss these challenges with me when she heard I was also a Christian like her.

Jane's story is a familiar one to many Christians. Many Christians have found that immediately they became regenerated (born again) through the New Birth in Christ Jesus, challenges, attacks, and confrontations that were not there before, suddenly sprang up. In fact, you might have been passing through similar situations in your life right now. Such experiences have caused many young born again Christians to abandon their faith and go back to their former unbelieving state.

The question, therefore, is: Why such opposition? Where does such opposition come from? What is the essence of such confrontations?

Interestingly, I took out time to go through the Scriptures with Jane. I told Jane, *"Flies will not perch on hot food, and cockroaches do not climb the surface of a red hot iron."*

The day you become regenerated (born again) in Christ, you enter into a war. It is a non-physical war. It is the age-old war between good and evil!

> *"For we wrestle not against flesh and blood, but against principalities, against powers, against the rulers of the darkness of this world, against spiritual wickedness in high places"*
>
> *(Eph.6:12 KJV)*

"For our fight is not against flesh and blood, but against principalities, against powers, against the rulers of the darkness of this world, and against spiritual forces of evil in the heavenly places" *(Eph.6:12 MEV)*

Satan and his demons are real personalities and they hate you because you have left their camp when you become born again and, therefore, no longer a member of their Kingdom of Darkness. These negative forces wage relentless battles against Christians. Most of the misfortunes, struggles, and disfavour like the ones that Jane suffered immediately she experienced the New Birth in Christ, were attacks and manipulations from the Satanic forces. Jane's boss and co-workers were only tools of manipulation by these Satanic forces to frustrate Jane.

The target of these forces was to pull Jane back from her faith. No king will want to lose his subjects to a rival kingdom. The Kingdom of God in which born-again Christians belong is the rival of the Satanic Kingdom of Darkness, and Satan with his demons will never want to lose any of his subjects to the rival Kingdom of God. Hence, they will do all they can, often through their *CDC devices* (see Page 170), to win back the born-again Christian.

Satan and demons are negatively intelligent beings. They knew by attacking Jane's sources of income, they could frustrate her. Thus, they launched attacks against Jane at her place of work. Never doubt this, Satan and demons are real beings with intelligence. They know when and how to attack, through their *CDC devices*. It often gives me concern whenever I hear some people claim Satan and demons do not exist. Of course, one of the demonic ploys is deception; deceiving the ignorant that they do not exist, hence, making them gullible and vulnerable to attack. SSB Book 1 dissects and analyses in detail the reality of the spiritual existence, and will be quite invaluable to read it along with this book.

Satan and demons with their human agents are the flies and the cockroaches that infest their human victims. If you are not in Christ, you are dust-food for them, for they can choose to do with you any how they want (Gen.3:14; see Page 155). Most of the sufferings, diseases, heartaches, pains, frustrations, ill-luck, disasters, et cetera, are products of these demonic attacks.

If you are regenerated in Christ, the way to keep demonic forces off your life and your environments is by heating up your faith into a red-hot iron.

"above all, taking the shield of faith, with which you will be able to extinguish all the fiery arrows of the evil one" (Eph.6:16 MEV).

"For whatever is born of God overcomes the world. And this is the victory that has overcome the world—our faith" (1Joh.5:4 NKJV).

"the just shall live by his faith"
(Hab.2:4; Rom.1:17; Gal.3:11; Heb.10:38 KJV).

If you are in Christ, you have authority by faith over these negative forces; they are under your feet (Rom.16:20; Eph.1:15-23). You can take the battles to their camp, disarm them successfully and suffer no harm, 'for nothing shall by any means harm you.

Behold, I give you the authority to trample on serpents and scorpions, and over all the power of the enemy, and nothing shall by any means hurt you" (Luk.10:19 NKJV).

However, the exercise of your authority in Christ by faith comes via knowledge. The more you know who you are in Christ and of your authority as a citizen of the Kingdom of God, the more you'll take control of the situations of your life, and drive off these spiritual flies and cockroaches. However, a Christian who does not know his authority will become a victim and suffer defeat.

"My people are destroyed for lack of knowledge" (Hos.4:6 NKJV).

For Jane, I invited her to Church, Living Faith also known as Winners Chapel, in Pretoria, where I worship. She joined the Church, started hearing faith-filled messages and reading faith-based Christian books that skyrocketed her spiritual stamina. She came to understand the authority of audacity of faith that changed everything for her. Eventually, she left her job, secured a better employment, and her private business picked up astronomically. She then began to live a faith-filed life, discovering a new world of victory.

OGOJA: THE TWELVE-YEAR-OLD BOY

Satan and the demons are real; they're not imaginative, theological discussions. In my practice of medicine, I have come across a number of such occurrences of demonic manipulations. The issues of some of these patients were direct attacks and manipulations by demonic forces. When medical therapy failed, I'd point some of these patients (those who were willing for such knowledge) to the reality of solutions in Christ Jesus, the Greatest Physician. Those that embraced the salvation offer in Christ always came back with smiles because of finally finding solutions for their problems.

Ogoja was a twelve-year-old boy admitted in the Paediatric Ward of our hospital during my internship. He had developed complications of tuberculosis, which had affected his spinal bone causing kyphosis, which appeared as 'hunch back.' He was bent forward when walking. In addition, he suffered from severe anemia (low blood level) because of concurrent infections that weakened him.

I remember clearly how he looked like a nine-year-old child due to the chronically debilitating condition. His sister, who was ten years, was looking much bigger and stronger. Ogoja had been sick for a long time, and his parents took him around various native herbalists and prayer houses seeking for a solution. By the time he was brought to the hospital, he had lost so much weight, became stunted in growth, and quite anaemic. His case was a very bad one and prognosis very poor. The medical doctors battled frantically to save his life. By the time I was posted in for our three-monthly rotation to join the team, Ogoja had spent about a week in the Paediatric Ward of the hospital.

Even if he had successfully been treated for the complicated tuberculosis, Ogoja might never walk straight again because of the hunch back. Spinal corrective surgery was far too expensive for Ogoja's family, and moreover, they were even struggling to pay the present medical bills.

The day I joined the team was a consultant ward round. As usual, nothing serious was done during the ward round for Ogoja because of the financial handicap the family was in. As we left Ogoja's ward to go to the next ward, my heart was so heavy in sorrow for such a young boy, wondering to myself how I could help him. At the door of the ward, I turned round to look at Ogoja and the pathetic parents by his bedside. As I did so, the Holy Spirit abruptly interjected my thought: *"Teach him some of the things you know."* These were clear words from the Spirit of God in my heart, and I undoubtedly knew they were from Him.

Immediately these words came into my heart, what to teach Ogoja and how to teach him just appeared clearly in my mind; it was like looking at itemised writings on a classroom board. I jotted them down immediately in my ward-round pocket jotter.

When the ward round had ended that day and I had finished my ward work, I strolled down to Ogoja's bedside. His parents were still there.

"Sir, I'd like to teach your son a couple of things for the next few days," I told the father, trying to obtain his consent.

"What could that be?" Ogoja's father asked in Pidgin English, which is commonly spoken in West and Central Africa.

"I'd like to teach him some things I believe will help his faith and his illness," I replied.

"Oh, a Christian teaching! Not a problem at all," the father said with anguish tone.

Ogoja's family attended a traditional Church, and from my interaction with them, they were not born again Christians, but merely nominal Church goers.

That day I taught Ogoja the **Power of Imagination**. I told him the story of the Tower of Babel in Genesis chapter eleven verses one to nine. I told him one of the positive lessons there was that these Babel builders pictured the Tower in their minds and hence could work tirelessly to actualise the pictures in their minds. I taught him to start picturing his health, his going back to school, as a grown-up man and a very successful accountant (he had earlier told me he wanted to be an accountant). I would encourage him to close his eyes and picture himself achieving all these.

Children easily pick these things fast. He would close his eyes and do exactly as I told him. When he pictured himself in that light, I would see smile around his face! That is the power of imagination. It was a Monday afternoon. I asked him to practise this as many times as possible each day for one week, especially first thing when he woke up and last thing before he slept.

Each day, I would stop by his bedside to ask him if he had practised the simple exercise, and truly he was doing it punctiliously to the extent that he had come to immensely enjoy the exercise and especially the pictures he envisioned.

Monday Second Week:
Again, after my ward round and ward work, I pulled a chair and sat by Ogoja's bedside. I taught him the **Power of Words**. I showed him and elaborated to him what the Bible means by:

> *"Death and life are in the power of the tongue, and those who love it will eat its fruit" (Pro.18:21 NKJV).*

I taught Ogoja at the level he would understand as a child the force of our words. I told him to start declaring positively faith-filled words like: *"I am healthy. I am back to school. I am going to be a successful accountant. Jesus is with me and He has healed me. I am healed and*

I am a blessing to my father, mother, sister, and the world. I am rich and very prosperous all round, etc." I literally filled his mind with words of faith. I charged him up to start speaking forth what he saw whenever he did the mental exercises I gave him the previous week. I encouraged him not to be ashamed or afraid of any person but to keep declaring those words. What an interesting child! Ogoja believed me and went about doing just that for the next one week.

Like the previous week, I'd stop by his bedside every day to ask him how he had been going about the exercises, and would rouse up his faith.

Monday Third Week:
On this day, after my usual consultant ward round and ward work, I taught Ogoja how to pray. I taught him that God is a Person. He should see God as a Big Loving Father, who was very willing to help him. I taught him the **Power of Thanksgiving and Praise** in prayer, simplifying the teaching in the way he could understand it. I taught him to begin to thank God for healing him of all his diseases. I explained to him why he should thank God even when he had not seen any physical evidence of healing. Finally, I led him and the family to salvation and receiving of Jesus as their Lord and Saviour.

In the course of this week, the parents noticed that Ogoja was no longer downtrodden and downcast as before. His conditions had not changed, but he was joyous. In fact, Ogoja's condition appeared to have even become more critical. We had to transfuse him with some units of blood. The poor father donated his blood. However, the haemoglobin (blood) level went down again despite the transfusion. Hence, we started investigating the cause of the persistent anaemia.

Notwithstanding, I encouraged Ogoja to practise what I taught him for the next week. As usual, I would stop by his bedside to give him words of encouragement.

Monday Fourth Week:
On this day, I taught Ogoja the **Power of the Holy Spirit.** I told him that the Holy Spirit is a Person, and He is the carrier of the power of God. I told him the Holy Spirit has been living in him from that day he had accepted Jesus as his Lord and Saviour.

In fulfilment of James chapter 5 verses 14 and 15, I then did something that appeared strange to Ogoja's parents. I gave the sister some money to buy some olive oil from across the hospital gate. I explained the Scriptures of James chapter 5 verses 14 and 15 to Ogoja and his family:

> *"Is anyone among you sick? Let him call for the elders of the church, and let them pray over him, anointing him with oil in the name of the Lord. And the prayer of faith will save the sick, and the Lord will raise him up. And if he has committed sins, he will be forgiven" (Jam.5:14,15 NKJV).*

I informed the family I would pray the prayer of faith over Ogoja as stated in the above Scriptures, representing the elders of my Church, Living Faith also known as Winners Chapel. I asked Ogoja to kneel down in reverence to God while I prayed the prayer of faith over him, and anointed him with the olive oil the sister had brought, as instructed by the Scriptures. Thereafter, I left.

Tuesday Fourth Week:
Something dramatic happened as I came to the ward in the morning after the previous day's prayer of faith. Ogoja, his parents and sister literally ran towards me in ecstasy, embracing and clinging to me. The nurses, who had been calling me Pastor all this while, were all jubilant. The whole ward was in a jubilant mood. I quickly looked down at the back of Ogoja, and the hunch back had disappeared. I stood there speechless as the import of what I just saw dawned on me. I took Ogoja aside to his bed and examined him thoroughly. He looked much healthier. His skin looked quite fresh. I checked for signs of anaemia, and lo and behold there was none. I checked for

the usual generalised lymphadenopathy (swellings around his neck and armpits), and like a dream, they were all gone.

I decided to draw his blood for more laboratory checks, and sent him for controlled X-rays. The laboratory results were all normal and no evidence of kyphosis (hunch back) on the X-rays was visible again. The senior doctors (the Registrar and Senior Registrar) came and confirmed the conditions. To them, this was too good to be true. The Senior Registrar informed the Consultant, who was the head of our Team.

Wednesday Fourth Week:
The Consultant came in the morning. He examined Ogoja and checked our clinical, laboratory and radiological findings. All were beyond medical explanation, considering the previous records.

"*I really don't understand,*" quipped the Consultant.

"*May be it's one of the so-called miracles,*" the Consultant mused.

The Consultant was not a Christian, and several times he would mock Christians as 'faith people that deceive people.' He did not know what had transpired between Ogoja and me in the past three and half weeks.

"*We can discharge him [Ogoja] for follow-up in our outpatient department,*" he finally instructed.

Meanwhile, being the most junior doctor (I was a fresh graduate from the medical school), I was standing at the back, giggling excitedly. One of the nurses could not help but blurted out: "*Praise the Lord,*" and I echoed "*Halleluiah!*"

"*What was that?*" my Consultant enquired absentmindedly.

Thus, Ogoja was discharged. Before he left, I went over to his bedside. I explained to him and his family what happened.

"*Jesus Christ has healed Ogoja,*" I told the family. "*Do not go back in your Christian faith. As you return to your village, locate a Bible-based Church to be attending,*" I advised. "*But if you go back in your faith and commitment to Jesus, Satan and his demons can come back to re-afflict Ogoja, and he might even be worse this time,*" I warned them.

They were from Ogoni in Rivers State of Nigeria. I knew of Assemblies of God in that region, hence, I recommended the Church, Assemblies of God, for them. In those days (year 2000), telephone was not common and GSM phones were not readily available in Africa, hence, I could not follow-up on Ogoja.

SYLVIA AND THE DEMONIC ATTACKS

The truth is that Satan and the demons hate humanity and often seek to destroy them, using principally ignorance, diseases, and poverty.

In April 2018, 23-year-old Sylvia came to our Clinic. The Clinic was always very busy each day, and patients would be allocated to the clinicians to attend to them. To be able to pick Sylvia out of the huge crowd that came to the clinic that day could only be by divine arrangement. At the end of the visit, Sylvia knew our meeting was not accidental or a chance occurrence, rather it was divinely arranged.

Sylvia was a born-again Christian. Sadly, she left the faith and entered into an illicit sexual relationship with a man. During that period, she started sensing some strange feeling around her and would occasionally hear a female voice. Soon the voce became frequent and she started seeing the personality behind the voice. It was a middle-aged woman, who would appear to her and issued commands that Sylvia often felt powerless to resist. When she mumbled some feeble resistance, the woman would curse and inflict physical pains on her.

Sylvia, who was a law student, couldn't focus on her studies any longer. She never had any psychiatric illness before and there was no known family history of mental disorder. Sylvia had never used any hard drugs nor had she ever smoked. As her condition degenerated, the family despatched a vehicle to bring her back from Pretoria, where she studied, to their home at Kwazulu Natal, a distance of about 620 kilometres. That day, something remarkable happened. The invisible woman immediately appeared to Sylvia to warn her not to go to Kwazulu Natal. However, Sylvia insisted she would travel.

On the same day that the family despatched a vehicle to fetch Sylvia, two men appeared in Pretoria to inform Sylvia that they were sent by her family. However, deep within her, Sylvia was not convinced; the two men looked strange. What saved her was that the mother, apparently trying unsuccessfully to reach her, left a message with a neighbour, who quickly got through to Sylvia. When the two men knew that their identity was uncovered, they drove off suddenly. Who were those two men? Apparently, their intention was evil. How did they know Sylvia was to travel to Kwazulu Natal that day? These were questions that neither Sylvia nor her family were able to answer.

Sylvia finally joined the transport sent by her mother to Kwazulu Natal. At her home in Kwazulu Natal, Sylvia was continuously being traumatised by the repeated apparitions. She was taken to a hospital, where she was tranquilised, which never really helped her because as soon as the tranquilisation effect waned off, Sylvia's affliction would resume.

Soon she started noticing a snake-like figure crawling behind her and she would occasionally fall on the floor wriggling like a snake.

For almost two years, Sylvia and her family spent time, energy, and resources seeking for a solution, both medically and spiritually. They visited psychologists, psychiatrists, and herbalists/spiritualists, but the symptoms got worse. She was traumatised far beyond measure, dejected, loathsome, and hopeless.

It was during such a moment that she visited our Clinic. On hearing her story, I knew it was a demonic attack. Sylvia had exposed herself to demonic influence by engaging in an illicit sexual activity after she had been born again.

"whoever breaks through a wall may be bitten by a snake"
(Ecc.10:8 NIV).

By dabbling into the sinful act, Sylvia had broken the hedge, the wall of divine protection, around her and the Serpent has struck. Satan and his demons are real personalities; they were the ones tormenting Sylvia. Their work is to *"steal and kill and destroy"* (Joh.10:10 NIV). They often attack when you are at the verge of a breakthrough. Sylvia was in her last year at the varsity to finish her law degree study, and the demons were all out to destroy her.

I recommended Spirit, Soul and Body – a Concise Analysis of Human Nature (SSB Book 1), which is the first book in this SSB Series. I let her to know why she needed to pray to God to forgive her sins and I encouraged her to rededicate her life to Jesus.

As her knowledge of the Word of God in the Scriptures increased and her faith soared up, Sylvia started to confront those demonic attacks. Abruptly, they stopped occurring. She returned to school, finished her course, and moved on triumphantly in her career. What medical knowledge could not achieve, her faith in Jesus did!

TOPE AND THE DEMONIC POSSESSION

Tope was born into an affluent family. He could afford all the good things in life; driving an elegant car while a university student, an achievement quite uncommon in Africa. On campus, he joined a club of other young men that exposed him to occultism. He enjoyed the prestige of being called a 'big boy' on campus, which his cult membership had offered him. Sadly, he didn't know he was walking into a Satanic trap.

As his cult involvement became deepened, he soon realised he had little regard for mercy and compassion, which were valuable qualities of our humanity. He would become excessively violent for flimsy reasons. According to him, he had participated in operations that involved maiming lives especially when a girlfriend of any member of his cult switched boyfriends. In such operations, they would pour acid on the girl's face to permanently disfigure her and even cut off the limbs of the new boyfriend.

He rose in rank in the cult to become a fearful personality on campus so that his name became a secret terror on campus for both students and lecturers. He utilised the terror and the name of his cult to sail through the first three years in his studies, as he and his cult would threaten the lecturers to award unmerited marks.

However, nemesis soon caught up with him. One of the lecturers reported his threats officially to the Senate of the university and he was expelled. His affluent parents, who did not know about the deep involvement of their son in the cult, were disappointed. However, through their connections, admission in another university was soon secured for Tope to finish his education.

It was at this stage that the parents started noticing some strange spiritual developments around Tope. They noticed that Tope could not concentrate on his studies. He constantly heard voices and saw strange faces. Occasionally, they would eavesdrop on Tope while he communicated with these unseen personalities. Their initial reaction was that Tope was becoming a psychiatric case. After much persuasion, Tope was taken to a psychiatrist for assessment and therapy. However, the psychiatrist did not find any features suggestive of psychiatric or psychological disorders with Tope.

Unknown to the parents, Tope would communicate with personalities, whom Tope claimed were 'dead people.' He could see into the world of the spirit, performed 'soul travel,' and exercised some level of control over his victims. Interestingly, Tope did not know they were demonic spirits he was communicating with. As usual, the demons completely deceived Tope about who they were.

It was during one of those 'soul travels' that Tope was struck down by the power of the Holy Spirit while he attempted to spiritually challenge a group of Christians on campus. On realising such a higher power, he came to Church to surrender his life to Jesus. He looked unkempt, tired, and frail that Sunday morning. We all listened and wondered at his testimony. In the course of the Sunday worship, he fell on the ground and started wriggling. The demons that possessed him were reacting to the presence of the power of

God. At the end, the prayer band members of the Church, of which I was one, took him aside and cast out the demons from him.

After the exorcism, Tope found a new lease of life. His joy was boundless as he surrendered completely to Jesus. Already, he knew about the reality of the spiritual world, hence, with such zest he plunged himself into the study of the Bible. His faith in Christ grew. I watched delightedly the progressive metamorphosis of Tope's life as his spiritual commitment in Christ deepened more and more. He finished his education, and became very committed in his Christian walk.

The point here is that Satan and the demons are real. Indeed, it is actually surprising to me when people claim Satan and demons were not real. In truth, these forces of darkness do work through the minds of humans to deceive humanity and afflict their victims due to such ignorance.

Sin is the life of Satan, and it stands in stark opposite to zoe, the life of God. Sin enslaves people as it did to Tope. Only the blood of Jesus can wash away sins, and the authority in the name of Jesus can overpower the evil of Satanic stronghold on a person's life, and that was what happened in Tope's life. Tope had experienced the zoe life of God; he had been translated from the Kingdom of Darkness into the Kingdom of God. That can be your story today if you will also surrender to Jesus Christ as your Lord and Saviour.

CHAPTER 29

THE PROMISED RESTORATION OF MAN

DESPITE THE PERPETUATING EVIL ON earth during the first 4000 years of human existence, orchestrated by the loss of man's Dominion Mandate, the *love of God* (known as *agape* in the Greek New Testament Bible) would not allow the Creator to close His eyes permanently to the plight of man. Despite that man ceased to be God's children and became children of Satan, yet the truth still remained that humans were created by God; they are the works of His hand. His agape love for the works of His hand would not allow God to turn His face altogether from the cries of man. In His sovereignty, God kick-started a program of restoration to salvage man from his lost hope.

THE PROMISED SEED

Due to His heart of agape love, right in the Garden of Eden, in the same day that the first humans (Adam and Eve) fell, God had decreed the restoration of the divine disorder through the coming of the Seed of the Woman.

"And I will put enmity
Between you and the woman,
And between your seed and her Seed;
He shall bruise your head,
And you shall bruise His heel" (Gen.3:15 NKJV).

The redemption of man and, hence, the restoration of the divine order on earth, would, therefore be by the activities of this Promised Seed of the Woman.

THE REDEMPTIVE ACTION OF THE PROMISED SEED

(a) Crush the head of the Serpent

The Promised Seed of the woman will be the One that will crush the head of the Serpent, that old Devil, who is Satan. That is, the Promised Seed will be the one that will defeat Satan and retrieve the stolen divine Dominion Mandate of Man.

(b) Recreation of New Species of Humans

After the defeat of Satan, the Promised Seed will then be the means by which new sons of God of human origin will be recreated to populate the earth. The Promised Seed will be the template for the recreation of man and restoration of the divine order in the universe. It is much like the production of protein in which a template called messenger RNA is required. Without the template, production of protein cannot take place. In the same way, without the Promised Seed, there won't be any production of new species of mankind and no restoration of the lost order in the universe. The success of the Promised Seed will, therefore, determine the success of the divine plan for man's recreation.

In chemistry, the Promised Seed can be likened to the substrate by which a chemical reaction is initiated to obtain the desired product. The desired products, in this case, are the new species of mankind that will carry no sin-genome in their nature. Thus, the Promised Seed would be the *scapegoat* by which the new species of humans would be produced.

(c) Restoration of Divine Order

The ultimate divine design in crushing the head of Satan and recreation of a new species of man is to restore the universe into the perfect order that God had initially intended. The purpose of God must stand. Satan, the demons, and the fallen humanity cannot thwart the counsel and purpose of God.

TWO IMPORTANT CRITERIA FOR THE PROMISED SEED

To be able to execute the above threefold functions, viz. crush the head of Satan, recreate a new human species, and restore the divine order in the world, the Promised Seed must meet two criteria:

• He must be the Seed of the Woman:

The Promised Seed would have to be born of a woman; He must be the Seed of the woman. In other words, the Promised Seed must be human. It had to be a human that could contend with Satan and get back the lost authority of man. This is in consonance with the Law of Existence, which states that 'each is after its kind' (Gen.1:11,12,21).

Angels are not humans, hence, they were not qualified to advocate and contend with Satan for the lost Dominion Mandate of Man, and be the template for recreation of new species of humans. Likewise, no other beings, other than humans, was qualified to be the template. According to the Law of Existence, only a human being was qualified to be the template for crushing the head of Satan, recreate the new species of man, and restore the divine order.

• The Promised Seed must be able to expunge out Satan's life from man's nature:

Sin is the life of Satan. It would take the superior zoe life to expunge out the sin-genome from the human nature. In other words, the coming Seed of the woman must not be contaminated by the life of Satan, sin. Rather, the coming Seed must carry the zoe life with which the sin-genome would be expunged from the human life. Zoe is superior to sin. It must be life for life; zoe life to replace sin life.

THE DILEMMA

The question, therefore, arose: who among humans was qualified?

Sadly, none among the sons of men was qualified. No human was qualified because the sin-genome from Satan had been transmitted down from Adam and Eve, the human progenitors. The whole of humanity inherited the sin-genome from Adam and Eve.

"All have sinned and fall short of the glory of God"

(Rom.3:23 NKJV).

What about other beings like angels? Were they not qualified to be the Promised Seed? Sadly, the Law of Existence totally disqualified them. As mentioned above, other beings such as angels were not qualified because their lives were not of the same order and kind like the human life.

Thus, the dilemma question remained: How would the above two criteria be met? How would a Seed be born by a woman and at same time carry no sin-genome?

In a grandiose, solemn meeting, in which all of creation was summoned before God, the Divine Plan for man's restoration was unveiled before the entire realms of creation. The Almighty God, the Creator of the Universe, posed the question: 'Whom shall I send?'

"Then I heard the voice of the Lord, saying, "Whom shall I send, and who will go for Us?" (Isa.6:8 AMP).

From all logical points of view, none in the entire realms of creation was worthy and qualified. None met the two criteria to be sent as the Promised Seed for the redemption of man and restoration of Satan-orchestrated disorder in the universe. All seemed hopeless! All seemed gloomy!

Realising this seeming hopelessness, Satan rejoiced exceedingly, believing that he had forever scored a decisive win against the Creator of the universe.

However, God is omniscient and omnipotent; *"Is anything too hard for Him?"* (Gen.18:14 KJV). God knew exactly what He would do. In His omniscient wisdom, He knew exactly what He would do to meet the two criteria for man's salvation.

GROWTH PHENOMENON – THE WISDOM OF THE GOD

On the same day Adam and Eve fell, God did something that the angels, Satan, and demons gasped at with surprise. From the skin of an animal, the Lord God made a beautifully splendid clothing for Adam and Eve to cover their nakedness!

"And the Lord God made clothing from animal skins for Adam and his wife" (Gen.3:21 NLT)

This was a significant feat in the history of fallen humanity. As children in Sunday School, when we studied the story of Adam and his wife, Eve, the first humans to arrive on earth, the first thing that became obvious was their nakedness. The Bible did not state how long Adam and Eve roamed about in nakedness before they were clothed, but it was in the same day of the Fall.

"Adam and his wife were both naked, and they felt no shame"
(Gen.2:25 NIV)

Why did God not teach them to make cloths to cover their nakedness? Why did God not make them with the full knowledge of production of goods? But such questions are borne out of ignorance of the ways and dealings of God. In all of His creative works, God never made any living organism with full maturity. In His omniscience and sovereignty, God builds in a **Growth Phenomenon** in all living organisms. All living organisms, including man, must grow into maturity. That is part of the Law of Existence; it is the wisdom of God in display! Every plant, just as every animal, must grow. You put a bean seed into the soil, waters it, and after a few days, it germinates, shoots out its cotyledons, then its leaves, and finally into a full blade of a bean plant that grows to bear bean fruits with their seeds. How this growth phenomenon occurs still remains grossly unexplained even with our modern scientific knowledge.

In the same manner, all parts of the human being (the spirit man, the soul [mind], and the body) are made to grow. God created the human spirit with his mind to grow just as He had formed the physical body of man to grow. Just as the physical body grows from babyhood, through infanthood, toddler, adolescence, and adulthood, the same way the human spirit and the mind are meant to grow in phases into maturity. That was the divine expectation from the first humans, Adam and Eve.

Sadly, the enemy, Satan, intercepted the growth phases of this couple. Satan knew the Laws of God because he was once the Covering Cherub, the archangel Lucifer in charge of the Laws of God. Satan knew Adam and his wife would definitely grow to a point where they would discover cloths to cover their nakedness. But Satan wanted to turn the situation into his own favour; he wanted such growth to come by his own terms and not as instituted by God. In other words, since his plan had been to dethrone God and become the Most High, Satan twisted the Law of God for his selfish ambition. He instigated Adam and Eve to disobey God by eating the forbidden fruit, which ultimately opened their eyes to their nakedness.

To show that Satan's method never results in anything good, Adam and Eve ate the forbidden fruit and their eyes did open to see their nakedness; but that was all Satan could do. He was unable to help this couple make clothing to cover their nakedness. Rather, by obeying Satan they ran into shame!

A SIGN OF WHAT WOULD BE COMING!

On the other hand, on the same day that man fell and became the child of Satan, the agape love of God compelled God to do the unthinkable – He killed an animal and made clothing for Adam and Eve! He was not under any obligation to do that. He could have chosen to discard Adam and Eve, just banish them to Hell since they now had the sin-genome in them like Satan and the demons. But He never did that. The agape love in His heart compelled Him to come to man's rescue. He killed an animal, and extracted the animal skin to produce cloths for sinful Adam and Eve.

The angels communed among themselves, but could not understand the mind of the Almighty. Satan and the demons stood in awe, completely oblivious to the working of the Creator as He clothed the fallen Adam and his wife, Eve.

However, unknown to the angels, Satan and the demons, by sacrificing the life of the animal and clothing the fallen Adam and Eve in the Garden of Eden, God was communicating an eternal message to humanity. It was a sign of what would be coming! The Promised Seed would sacrifice His life to cloth humanity from eternal shame. The Promised Seed would sacrifice His life for the redemption of mankind!

Therefore, by the events in the Garden of Eden, God emphatically established the fact that the Promised Seed would definitely come on earth for human rescue, else humanity would be doomed eternally to Hell, the home of Satan and demons. In other words, in the end, Good would conquer Evil in the ensuing Great Conflict, and the perfect divine order would be established all through the realms of creation.

Indeed, no matter how long it takes, Good ultimately triumphs over Evil. As moral agents, we have the ability to choose whether to be part of the Good or Evil. About 4000 years after the events that took place in the Garden of Eden, the Promised Seed came as it was foretold – a testimony of the continuously glorious conquest of the Evil by the Good! SSB Book 4 graphically captures the progressively unfolding historical accounts of humanity from the Garden of Eden that culminated in the fulfilment of this 4000 year-old prophecy – the coming of the Promised Seed in about 1 BC.

Bibliography

Andrews S. (2017) "The Colossus of Rhodes – One of the Seven Wonders of the Ancient World."[Online] Available from: https://www. thevintagenews. com/2017/05/11/the-colossus-of-rhodes-one-of-the-seven-wonders-of-the-ancient-world/ (Accessed: 28th December 2018).

BBC (1999) "World's Worst Killers." BBC News, Saturday, 30 October, 1999, 16:40 GMT. [Online] Available from: http://news. bbc. co. uk/2/hi/495477. stm (Accessed: 26 December 2018).

Beaver P. (1971). In: A History of Lighthouses. London: Peter Davies Ltd, pp. 10-11.

Bible Universe (2019) "Creation and Evolution." [Online] Available from: https://www. bibleuniverse. com/articles/creation-and-evolution (Accessed: 4th January 2019).

Blazeski G. (2017) "In Ancient Rome, a slave would continuously whisper 'Remember you are mortal'" [Online] Available from: https://www. thevintagenews. com/2017/01/23/in-ancient-rome-a-slave-would-continuously-whisper-remember-you-are-mortal-in-the-ears-of-victorious-generals-as-they-were-paraded-through-the-streets-after-coming-home-triumphant-from-battle/ (Accessed: 28 April 2018).

Bruemmer B. A. (1994). Politics and Culture in International History: From the Ancient Near East to the Opening of the Modern Age. Transaction Publishers. p. 108. [Online] Available from: https://books. google. co. za/books? id=9hwwEBfJC0YC&redir_esc=y (Accessed: 28th December 2018).

Cartwright M. (2018) "Statue of Zeus at Olympia." Ancient History Encyclopedia, 24 July 2018. [Online] Available from: https://www. ancient. eu/Statue_of_Zeus_at_Olympia/ (Accessed: 07 January 2019).

Clayton P. A. (2013). "Chapter 7: The Pharos at Alexandria." In: Peter A. Clayton; Martin J. Price. The Seven Wonders of the Ancient World. London: Routledge. p.11. [Online] Available from: https://books. google. co. za/books? id=UU2AAAAAQBAJ&redir_esc=y (Accessed: 29th December 2018).

CNN (2017) "Oldest Homo sapiens fossils discovered." Ashley Strickland, CNN – Cable News Network, 08 June 2017. [Online] Available from: *http:// edition. cnn. com/2017/06/07/health/oldest-homo-sapiens-fossils-found/ index. html* (Accessed: 08 August 2017).

Cicero M. Tullius (45 BC). In: De Natura Deorum (On the Nature of the Gods). [Online] Available from: http://www. perseus. tufts. edu/hopper/text? doc=urn:cts:latinLit:phi0474. phi050. perseus-lat1:2.7 (Accessed: 28th December 2018).

Dio Chrysostom (AD 97). In: Discourses – The Twelfth or Olympic Discourse: Or, On Man's First Conception of God. [Online] Available from: http:// penelope. uchicago. edu/Thayer/E/Roman/Texts/Dio_Chrysostom/ Discourses/12*. html#16 (Accessed: 07 January 2019).

Encyclopaedia Britannica (2018) "Hanging Gardens of Babylon." [Online] Available from: https://www. britannica. com/place/Hanging-Gardens-of-Babylon (Accessed: 06 January 2019).

Encyclopædia Britannica (2018) "Phidias: Greek Sculptor." [Online] Available from: https://www. britannica. com/biography/Phidias (Accessed: 29th December 2018).

English School (2014) "Statue Of Zeus At Oympia." [Online] Available from: https://pixels. com/featured/statue-of-zeus-at-oympia-english-school. html (Accessed: 06 January 2019).

Ephesus WS (2019) "Temple of Artemis." [Online] Available from: http:// www. ephesus. ws/temple-of-artemis. html (Accessed: 06 January 2019).

Explore Turkey (2018). "St. Sophia: Construction for the Third Time." [Online] Available from: https://www. exploreturkey. com/exptur. php? id=176 (Accessed: 29th December 2018).

Fleagle J., Assefa Z., Brown F., and Shea J. (2008). "Paleoanthropology of the Kibish Formation, southern Ethiopia: Introduction." Journal of Human Evolution, 55 (3): 360–365. [Online] Available from: *https://www. ncbi. nlm. nih. gov/pubmed/18617219* (Accessed: 12 August 2017).

Guymon B. (2018) "Mausoleum at Halicarnassus." [Online] Available from: https://kidspast. com/world-history/mausoleum-halicarnassus/ (Accessed: 29th December 2018).

Haas C. (1997). In: Alexandria in Late Antiquity: Topography and Social Conflict. Johns Hopkins.

Higgins R. (1988) "The Colossus of Rhodes." In: The Seven Wonders of the Ancient World, Peter A. Clayton and Martin Jessop Price (eds.). Psychology Press, p. 30.

Higonnet P. L., Tuppen N. J., Shennan H. J., et al (2018) "France." [Online] Available from: *https://global. britannica. com/place/France* (Accessed: 28 April 2018).

Hippocrates of Kos (c.400 BC) "The Hippocratic Oath: Classical Version." Translation from the Greek by Ludwig Edelstein. From The Hippocratic Oath: Text, Translation, and Interpretation, by Ludwig Edelstein. Baltimore: Johns Hopkins Press, 1943. [Online] Available from: https:// www. pbs. org/wgbh/nova/doctors/oath_classical. html (Accessed: 07 January 2019).

Jarus O. (2014) "Pyramids of Giza & the Sphinx." Live Science, October 9, 2014 09:24 pm ET. [Online] Available from: https://www. livescience. com/22621-pyramids-giza-sphinx. html (Accessed: 06 January 2019).

Jordan P. (2014). In: Seven Wonders of the Ancient World. Routledge. p. 44. [Online] Available from: https://books. google. co. za/books?id=LeN9AwAAQBAJ&pg=PA44&redir_esc=y (Accessed: 29th December 2018).

Josephus Flavius (c. AD 94). In: Antiquities of the Jews. The Works of Flavius Josephus; translated by William Whiston, A. M. Auburn and Buffalo. NY: John E. Beardsley, 1895. [Online] Available from: http://www. perseus. tufts. edu/hopper/text? doc=Perseus:text:1999.01.0146 (Accessed: 17 November 2017).

Kostof S. (1985). In: A History of Architecture. Oxford: Oxford University Press. p.9.

Lazenby J. F. (1978). Hannibal's War. Aris & Phillips.

Lendering J. (2017). In: ABC 5 (Jerusalem Chronicle). [Online] Available from: http://www. livius. org/sources/content/mesopotamian-chronicles-content/abc-5-jerusalem-chronicle/ (Accessed: 28th December 2018).

Livius Titus (9 BC). In: Ab Urbe Condita, XLV. 28, 5. Penguin translation by H. Bettenson. [Online] Available from: http://www. u. arizona. edu/~afutrell/republic/livy45week9. html (Accessed: 07 January 2019).

Mark J. J. (2016) "The Great Sphinx of Giza." Ancient History Encyclopedia; published on 26 October 2016. [Online] Available from: https://www. ancient. eu/The_Great_Sphinx_of_Giza/ (Accessed: 06 January 2019).

Meleager of Gadara (c.60 BC). In: Anthologia Graeca, vol.4, p.171. Edited by Hermann Beckby, Munich, 1957.

Miguel Civil (2011). "The Law Collection of Ur-Namma." In: Cuneiform Royal Inscriptions and Related Texts in the Schøyen Collection, 221–286, edited by A. R. George, 2011.

Nitecki M. H. and Nitecki D. V. (1994). In: Origins of Anatomically Modern Humans. Springer.

Pappas S. (2017) "'Living Fossils' of Earth's Oldest Life-Forms Found in Tasmania." Live Science, November 16, 2017 04:29pm ET. [Online] Available from: *https://www. livescience. com/60962-living-fossils-of-oldest-life-tasmania. html? utm_source=notification* (Accessed: 28 April 2018).

PBS (1997) "Treasures of the Sunken City." PBS Airdate: November 18, 1997. Nova. Season 24. Episode 17. Transcript. [Online] Available from: https:// www. pbs. org/wgbh/nova/transcripts/2417treasures. html (Accessed: 07 January 2019).

Rankov B. (2011). 'A War of Phases: Strategies and Stalemates 264–241." In: Hoyos, Dexter. A Companion to the Punic Wars. Oxford: Wiley-Blackwell.

Richter D., Grün R., Joannes-Boyau R., et al. (2017) "The age of the hominin fossils from Jebel Irhoud, Morocco, and the origins of the Middle Stone Age." Nature, 546, 293–296, 08 June 2017. [Online] Available from: *http://www. nature. com/nature/journal/v546/n7657/full/nature22335. html? foxtrotcallback=true* (Accessed: 08 August 2017).

Roth M. (1995). Law Collections from Mesopotamia and Asia Minor, pp. 13–22. [Online] Available from: http://www. g2rp. com/pdfs/ LawCollectionsFromMesopotemiaAndAsiaMinor. pdf (Accessed: 06 January 2019).

Schopf J. W. (1992). In: Major Events in the History of Life. Jones & Bartlett Learning. pp. 168–.

Scientific American (2005) "Fossil Reanalysis Pushes Back Origin of Homo sapiens." [Online] Available from: *https://www. scientificamerican. com/ article/fossil-reanalysis-pushes/* (Accessed: 08 August 2017).

Sheridan P. (2015) "The Sacred Chickens of Rome." Anecdotes from Antiquity. [Online] Available from: http://www. anecdotesfromantiquity. net/the-sacred-chickens-of-rome/ (Accessed: 28th December 2018).

Strabo (AD 23). In: The Geographica, Book XIV. The Loeb Classical Library edition, 1928. [Online] Available from: http://penelope. uchicago. edu/ Thayer/E/Roman/Texts/Strabo/home. html (Accessed: 28th December 2018).

Toynbee J. A. (2018) "Julius Caesar – Roman Ruler." [Online] Available from: *https://global. britannica. com/biography/Julius-Caesar-Roman-ruler* (Accessed: 28 April 2018).

Wasson L. D. (2012) "Battle of Gaugamela." Ancient History Encyclopedia. [Online] Available from: https://www. ancient. eu/Battle_of_Gaugamela/ (Accessed: 28th December 2018).